AN UNFINISHED
AUTOBIOGRAPHY

THE WARDEN: NEW COLLEGE, 1940
(*from a photograph by Howard Coster*)

H. A. L. Fisher

===

AN UNFINISHED AUTOBIOGRAPHY

WITH A FOREWORD BY
LETTICE FISHER

OXFORD UNIVERSITY PRESS
LONDON   NEW YORK   TORONTO
1940

OXFORD UNIVERSITY PRESS
AMEN HOUSE, E.C. 4
London Edinburgh Glasgow New York
Toronto Melbourne Capetown Bombay
Calcutta Madras
HUMPHREY MILFORD
PUBLISHER TO THE UNIVERSITY

PRINTED IN GREAT BRITAIN

Foreword

THESE memoirs were begun within a few weeks of the outbreak of war in September '39. The Warden had little leisure. Not only undergraduates and dons, but New College men of every generation, and indeed men and women of all kinds and all ages sought from him advice and consolation. There was endless college and university business, all the reorientation and reorganization necessitated by the hateful transition from peace to war. The Warden, with his long and profound experience of administration and affairs, was an inexhaustible source of help. From early morning till late at night the stream of inquirers flowed into his study: letters poured in from all over the world.

Amidst all these unhappy activities he determined to seek comfort in the recapture of old memories, and his ability to maintain that serenity and steadfastness, which all through the winter and spring so greatly comforted the endless people who came to him for help, was in part due to the dedication of his scanty leisure to these recollections of his youth, his family, and his friends.

The writing of the unfinished American chapter, upon which he was working at the time of his accident, had been suggested by his friends Logan Pearsall Smith and Ellery Sidgwick. Canada and the United States are full of our friends, and he greatly enjoyed his American experiences. We first crossed the Atlantic in 1909,[1] and again in '24, when he lectured in Canada, once more gave the Lowell lectures in Boston, and addressed a number of American colleges and universities. In 1930 he delivered to an immense audience gathered upon Boston Common the address commemorating the tercentenary of the city's foundation (published as *The Bay Colony*) and in 1935 he (with Sir Roger Keyes) represented the British Government at the celebrations of the discovery of Canada by Jacques Cartier. On this occasion he electrified his French-Canadian audiences by the wit, eloquence, and understanding of his French speeches. Finally, immediately after the Coronation we went to New York in order that he might receive an honorary degree from Columbia University.

The memoirs tell of his life up to the time when he became Modern History Tutor at New College. This position involved extremely hard work, for he taught all periods of English and European history, as well as some economics and political theory, much of which he had to learn in order to teach. Before long he embarked upon the historical research which materialized in his *Medieval Empire*, published at the end of 1898, and meanwhile contributed articles upon literary and historical subjects to the *Fortnightly*, the *English Historical Review*, and other periodicals. He was the outstanding figure among the younger Oxford dons. His lectures had an unusual bril-

---

[1] His Lowell lectures of that year were published as *The Republican Tradition in Europe,* 1910.

liance, he took part in many activities, lecturing to large audiences of working men from Oxford House in Bethnal Green, speaking in the Liberal interest at political meetings, advocating the admission of women to degrees, making himself an authority upon Dante, travelling abroad in the vacations, keeping in touch with a large, varied, and ever-growing circle of friends.

His powers of work were extraordinary. He gave unsparingly to his pupils, while at the same time he unremittingly pursued his historical studies, activities which continued after our marriage in 1899. In term time he used to pile all his teaching on to the end of the week, keeping the early days for research, and very much needing the relaxation of social life on Sundays. In the vacations he worked in the British Museum or in the Paris Archives or the Bibliothèque Nationale, or pursued the problem of the moment to German archives or to the libraries of Rome. Lord Acton had invited him to undertake the Napoleonic chapters of the Cambridge Modern History, and he soon became one of the leading authorities upon the Napoleonic period. Teaching, lecturing, writing not only upon Napoleon but upon the early Tudors, editing the works of his brother-in-law F. W. Maitland and writing his biography, acting as one of the editors of the Home University Library, researching in France, Germany, and Rome, with one exciting visit to Corsica, enjoying brief summer holidays in the Alps and visits to our respective families and friends, his days were full.

We went to South Africa in 1908, where he lectured

with great success, and to America in 1909. In 1912 he was asked by Lord Crewe to serve upon the Indian Public Services Commission, and he went to India in January 1913, a few days after the birth of our daughter. Meanwhile he had been offered, and had accepted, subject to the claims of the Indian Commission, the Vice-Chancellorship of Sheffield University. We spent the interval between the two Indian visits near Sheffield, learning something of the work and ways of a new university, and in the spring of 1914 left Oxford and established ourselves in the unknown world of the industrial north. Hardly had we begun to find our way about when the war was upon us. He took a leading part in every sort of war activity, civic and academic, served upon the Bryce Committee of inquiry into German atrocities in Belgium, was sent to France to inquire into British propaganda. He has himself described how he was called from all this to join Mr. Lloyd George's Government in December 1916.

With Lord Balfour he represented Great Britain upon the League of Nations during the first three years of its existence. His service upon Council and Assembly was not only work which his command of languages, his wide knowledge of Europe, and his great social gifts enabled him to perform with outstanding success, but also work which satisfied, interested, and absorbed him to the full.

When Mr. Lloyd George's Government went out of office in '22 he was suddenly out of work. Sheffield University had at first lent him to the Government, hoping that he would return after the war. But at the time of the 1918 election it was necessary to choose between the University and the Government, and we left Sheffield, where he was succeeded by our old friend Sir Henry Hadow. Lecturing, writing, and the House of Commons filled his time, but although leaving London and public life was a great wrench, he had little doubt as to the wisdom of accepting the Wardenship of his old college in 1925.

The Warden's Lodgings, with the Surrey cottage where we had settled on leaving Sheffield, made a perfect setting for the last fifteen years of his life. Thanks to Sir Henry Lunn we had various summer holidays at Mürren and Maloja, and some happy cruises with the Hellenic Travellers' Club, of which the Warden became President. The last period of his life was as full as the earlier had been, with college and university work, plenty of writing and speaking, acting as Principal of the City of London Vacation course for Teachers, helping to found and to guide the Oxford Preservation Trust, presiding over the British Academy and later over the London Library, acting as a Rhodes Trustee, in which capacity he devoted much time and thought to the building of Rhodes House, as a Trustee of the British Museum, as a Governor of the B.B.C. (an office in which he was particularly interested), as Governor of various schools, especially his dearly loved Winchester, of which he was a Fellow for many years, and as a member of countless bodies, literary, academic, and political. Beside all this he made a point of seeing as much as possible of the undergraduates and of making friends with them and with the rest of Oxford. Entertaining in the beautiful rooms of the Warden's Lodgings and displaying the college treasures were sources of great pleasure to him.

The writing of his great *History of Europe*, combined as it was with so many other activities and so many demands upon his strength, together with the darkening international outlook, proved too much for his strength, and he was obliged to take a thorough rest—the first in his life—during the first three months of 1936. He made, however, a complete recovery, returned to most if not quite all his old activities, and when the war came was especially pleased to find himself able to carry on not only his ordinary avocations, but also to undertake the chairmanship of the Appellate Tribunal for Conscientious Objectors, a delicate and difficult post which he filled to perfection. He was on his way to this Tribunal when he met the accident that caused his death.

LETTICE FISHER

August, 1940

Contents

List of Illustrations

My Family

I was born on March 21st, 1865, at 3 Onslow Square, a little white slip of a house which somehow or other has continued to survive the transformations of seventy years, and still awakes as I pass it the sweet and affectionate memories of my Victorian childhood. Was it not from those windows that we were taught to look out for Mr. Justice Byles riding to the Law Courts every morning on his white hack Bills, that we watched, being waked up specially by the nurse, the glorious conflagration of the Pantechnicon, and enjoyed over and over again the unending enchantment of Punch and Judy? From time to time we were warned that we should look carefully at two old gentlemen, Mr. Froude and Mr. Carlyle, as they strolled past the windows of No. 3, but their names meant little to us then, and save for a vague feeling that in some mysterious way, intelligible only to grown-ups, we were privileged by the contemplation of these aged creatures, I doubt whether the experience would ever have been recorded in my memory any more than those visits to the nursery of Marlborough House, where it was apparently our distinction to play with the most august babies in the land, all of which, but for the information subsequently supplied by the recording angel of a nurse, would have been as if they never were.

For during the first five years of my life my father happened to be acting as Private Secretary to the Prince

B

of Wales, a post which he held from 1860 to 1870. Little gusts of memory arising from this august connexion sweep into my mind as I write, the burden of my second name Albert, the handsome silver gilt christening cup from the royal godfather, the delight of watching with my sister, Florence, the Changing of the Guard from the gardens of Marlborough House, glimpses of my father attiring himself for a day with the Windsor Staghounds or walking after grouse with the Prince, and above all the happy summer holidays which we spent at Birkhall, which the Prince on more than one occasion was kind enough to put at the disposal of my parents. August in Scotland! Even to small children, who have not learned to pursue wild animals, what better playground? Little did we think of great personages and high politics. The nursery picnics were enough for us and the exciting preparations for the Ghillies Ball, which my mother opened by dancing with the gamekeeper while my father led out the cook, an arrangement which when I got to hear of it filled my heart with delight. For I thought the gamekeeper and the cook very great people, and far more interesting than the two Royal gentlemen who came in to tea one day after shooting and over whom my father and mother made such a fuss, apologizing as I thought with undue solicitude when I slapped one of them on the face and told him that he was a silly man.

Indeed, neither then nor as we grew older did we hear much from my father of his life at Court. Conversations about the Royal family were always strongly discouraged in the home circle, for my father felt that of all forms of gossip that was, especially in view of his confidential position, the least desirable. I know, however, that he held the Prince in great affection and regard, saying of him that though he was never able to persuade him to read a book or prepare a speech, he always managed to rise to the occasion and to say the right thing. As to his royal master's feelings towards him I can only recall an impression of kindness and consideration continuing through life. 'Handsome as ever, Fisher, I see', King Edward would say to him as he paid his annual duty at a levée, a story needless to say that was never told by my father himself.

Save that he was good looking and well mannered my father was the last person in the world for a Court life. His temperament was that of a scholar-poet, meditative, gentle, withdrawn, exquisitely fastidious in his personal and literary tastes. That he should have been connected with the Court was, I imagine, due to a pure accident. When the Prince Consort was looking about for a guide and mentor to supervise his eldest son's student days at Oxford and Cambridge he applied to Henry Liddell, the Dean of Christ Church. Now the Dean was one of my father's older friends, and though my father had left Oxford and was practising at the Bar, he submitted his name, as that of a distinguished young student of Christ Church, for the post, and my father being engaged to be married, and anxious for an immediate income, accepted the offer. The tutorship, however, was a very brief appointment, and but for the fact that the Prince Consort conceived a regard for my father, a regard which was warmly reciprocated, for my father had a great admiration for the Prince's intellect and character, would not have led to anything further. Indeed it was, I imagine, to my father's professional interest to devote his undivided attention to the Law and to persevere in a profession in which he was beginning to make some progress. But when the tutorship came to an end, the Prince Consort expressed a strong hope that should his son ever require my father's services again in another capacity, they would be forthcoming. So when a little later the office of Private Secretary came his way, my father felt under a certain obligation to accept it, deserted the pleasant life of circuit and chambers, married my mother, and embarked on a decade of service to the Prince.

It is only by slow degrees that a parent unfolds himself to a child. My early impressions of my father are those of a beautiful being, very vivid and fond of the open air, grudging every moment spent indoors when the weather was fine, a swift runner and a great promoter of races among children, always faultlessly neat, and as it seemed to us splendid in his dress. We heard of him hunting and shooting and going to grand dinners and balls, and skating at Sandringham when we wanted him at home, and we knew how indulgent he could be to us when we were allowed down to dessert before bed-time.

Later when we were older and had begun to do lessons we learned that my father was terribly clever. He had taken a First Class in Classics at Oxford, and could write Greek and Latin verse. I think, as I look back now, that my father was a beautiful scholar in the old Oxford sense of the term. He was not learned. He had no German. He made no effort to acquaint himself with the lesser known writers of antiquity, but the great classics, Homer, Aeschylus, Pindar, Virgil, he knew intimately and was able to communicate his love and admiration for their work to others. He had that 'vision of greatness' which should be the prize of any good system of education, and it was from his reading of Greek poetry that I derived when quite a child my appreciation of the fact that Greek was the key to a beautiful literature and not merely a tiresome task devised for the misery of children. From my own experience I should doubt whether any part of education can be so valuable to a child as that he should hear soon and often the great masterpieces of poetry from the lips of one who feels their beauty and can transmit it.

It was much later that I came to know anything of my father's family, for my uncles and aunts on my father's side were deeply buried in rusticity and very seldom crossed my childish path. But with my father as with most people family environment was all important, for he came of one of those cultivated families of the rural middle class which for centuries have been the mainstay of English social life. He was the son of a Canon of Salisbury, who, like his father (the Master of Charterhouse) before him, had been a Fellow of his Oxford College, and was born in the North Canonry in a charming old house in the Close, with a crypt of the thirteenth century and a long garden running down to the swirling waters of the Avon and Nadder. I cannot pretend that my Fisher ancestors were distinguished, though an unsubstantiated claim is made that the saint and martyr should figure on the family tree. But ever since the middle of the eighteenth century they were in a high degree respectable. Two of my father's relations, his great-uncle John Fisher, Bishop successively of Exeter and Salisbury, and his uncle John Fisher, Archdeacon of Berks., secured a modest niche in the Temple of Fame as having been early to discover, to befriend, and to reward the genius of Constable, and one Osmond Fisher, a cousin of my father's, distinguished himself greatly as a geologist, being the author of the *Physics of the Earth's Crust*, a classical treatise, crossing swords with Kelvin and combining in an unusual and happy harmony with his austere pursuits in physics and geology the expert skill of a rose grower and a pyrotechnician. There were others, soldiers and clergymen who did well in their several professions and who lie buried in quiet English churchyards or in India, a race of refined, retiring men, well content with a modest station in life, scholars, bird-lovers, landscape painters, and sportsmen, Anglicans all of them and orthodox in an old-fashioned way and English to the core. One of them after a century of oblivion begins to attract some notice from connoisseurs in art. The delicate water-colours of Major-General Sir George Bulteel Fisher, my father's great-uncle, emerge now and again from family portfolios and find their way into London salerooms.

Of the women of the family two only appear to have been remarkable, my grandmother, one of the Cooksons of Cumberland, and the first cousin of William Wordsworth the poet, and my aunt Emmeline, who had a great family reputation as an infant prodigy and as a poetess. In these days, no doubt, Aunt Emmeline's gifts would have been carefully tended and encouraged, but she was married as a girl to a poor Wiltshire clergyman and a few years later succumbed to the burdens of a family and a parish. A slender volume of poems by Emmeline Hinxman (Longmans, 1856, 2nd ed. 1857) preserves for posterity a modest rill of delicate Victorian sentiment.

> The thrush takes up her evening strain,
> O'er ringing fallows mounts the lark,
> The primrose stars the village lane
> And knolls and hollows of the park.

But whether under happier auspices the authoress of 'The Wraith', 'Moonlight Fancies', 'The Hall and The Cottage', and 'The Garden of Reverie', would ever have developed her easy gift for improvization into a real talent who can say? Wordsworth, the family mentor, was strongly opposed to the idea that his young friend should be encouraged in authorship. In a series of solemn letters he warned my grandmother against allowing her daughter to publish poetry or to train herself for anything but a career of domestic duty, and as Wordsworth was not an infrequent inmate in my grandmother's house ('Who is that old General staying with you?' asked the neighbours), he had many opportunities of reinforcing his written precepts by verbal monitions. Not that the old poet underrated the poetic genius of the girl. It is more likely that he thought of it too highly. Indeed, on one occasion, being required by Queen Victoria to rewrite the National Anthem on pacifist lines, and finding the task beyond him, the Laureate invited Emmeline Fisher, then a child of twelve, to step into the breach. Undaunted by the task of supplying the place of the Poet Laureate the young lady took up her pen and dashed off an anthem, which earned for her the warm acknowledgements of the poet and a silver inkstand from the Queen.

Of all this, however, I knew nothing as a child, and it was only by degrees that I realized my father's connexions with the poet, and heard how he walked over to Ullswater with an Oxford reading party to see him at Grasmere, and of how the provoking old man would talk of nothing but boots much to my father's chagrin, for he had hoped that his kinsman would show off to advantage to the clever company of young Christ Church friends whom he had brought over the fells to worship at the shrine.

Indeed, as I look back and reflect upon the paternal

side of my family, it is curious how little my father's relations entered into my life. My grandmother I could not have seen for she died in 1851, fourteen years before my birth. My grandfather, who died when I was nine years of age, I never remember to have seen. My uncles and aunts were at that stage of my life very shadowy figures, the most interesting (though I only remember to have seen him once) being my uncle Arthur, a Colonel of Engineers, who had served in the Crimea and who for that reason shone with a mysterious lustre. But in those days travelling was slow, difficult, and expensive, and as there was no family place which could serve as a rallying point for our widely scattered members, and my uncles and aunts were all busy people, we children saw them only on rare and distinguished occasions.

It was otherwise with my mother's side of the family. Here there was much to attract the imagination and curiosity of a child. There was France and the French Revolution, India and the jungle, beautiful and talented women, elderly men reported to be wise and famous. My mother was the second daughter of Maria Jackson, the fourth and as some would say the most lovely of the seven Pattle sisters who at one time created some stir in Victorian society by their good looks, warm hearts, and high-spirited and unconventional ways, and as our holidays were largely spent at Saxonbury Lodge, Kent, my grandfather's house, we could hardly escape learning something of that side of the family story or of meeting

C

from time to time one or other of our brilliant great aunts or of our grandparents' Anglo-Indian friends and relations. The family story was as follows:

At the court of Marie Antoinette was a very handsome, tall, and dashing page, Antoine de l'Étang, a fine horseman, a lavish spender, and distinguished throughout his life for a certain stately elaboration of manner which was no doubt a specific product of Versailles. Whether the Queen became too fond of the young gentleman, or whether the young gentleman was too attentive to the Queen we do not know. It is sufficient that rumour connected their names and that it was convenient to ship the young Chevalier to Pondicherry. There in 1788 he married a certain Mademoiselle Blin de Grincourt, by whom he had three daughters, the second of whom, Adeline, married one James Pattle of the Bengal Civil Service and became the mother of those seven Pattle sisters, who shimmered distantly at the circumference of my childish experience as great, beneficent, and generally incalculable beings. As for the Chevalier himself he was that elastic adaptable kind of Frenchman who finds his feet anywhere. He survived, an adventurer, turning defeat into opportunity, so that when the French cause was broken in India he made friends with the conquerors, and cut a dash in Calcutta society where he opened a riding school and practised as a veterinary surgeon. Horsemanship is everywhere a talisman, but more especially in India. The skill of the Chevalier became widely known outside the jurisdiction of John

Company. In 1814 he was elevated to the service of the Nawab of Oudh and so for another six-and-twenty years lived on schooling horses for Indian horsemen, a showy, exuberant, and, I imagine, slightly ostentatious figure, but a master of his craft, and popular with Indians and English alike. As for Madame de l'Étang, his widow, she lived on into my own lifetime, dying on January 5th, 1866, within three months of the hundredth year of her age, at No. 1 Place St. Louis, Versailles. For to Versailles she had returned after her husband's death, and there to this day, I believe, some distant members of my family may be found.

Of this French connexion my grandmother and my mother, who had received part of her education in France, were both proud. We often heard tell of our ancestor the Chevalier. Of our nearer relation James Pattle, 'the greatest liar in India', we learned little or nothing. Though we knew little of history we were made to feel that somehow it was an altogether grand and romantic thing to be connected through the Chevalier with the unfortunate French Queen who had lost her head on the scaffold. France seemed in a certain way to belong to us, so that when we learned of the war with Prussia through the pictures in the *Illustrated London News*, it was France not Germany which received support from our nursery. What, if any, French characteristics were communicated by the Chevalier to his descendants I cannot say. It can, however, seldom happen that the essential structure of a man's face is so faithfully transmitted to a long series of his descendants. The 'Pattle face' did not come from James Pattle, but was transmitted, as a visit to the Watts Gallery at Compton will show, through his wife Adeline from her father the Chevalier.

It was through my mother's side of the family again that India came to play a part in my early imaginings. Dr. Jackson, our grandfather, had spent all his active life in India in the service of John Company, and as the leading English physician in Calcutta had a wide circle of friends in British India and in the Native States who regarded him with grateful veneration. Seeing that during the first twenty-five years of his Indian service he had never once come home, and then only to find that his native Lincolnshire village was empty of all his relations and their friends and that his very existence had been completely forgotten, he was as deeply rooted in Indian soil as an Englishman can hope to be. His friends, his thoughts, his enjoyments were all connected with the country in which he had spent his working life and from which he had reaped a handsome fortune. And as from time to time our grandfather chattered in Hindustani or revived old memories with some Anglo-Indian visitor, we children, skirmishing along the fringes of a conversation of which we could understand only the merest fragments, were made to feel the presence of the mysterious East, with its peacocks and elephants, its temples and lakes, its veiled princesses and jewelled princes, and wondered why our grandparents had ever exchanged such splendours and delights for the quiet comforts of their Kentish home.

Nor were my grandparents the only Anglo-Indians who came into my childhood. Two of my mother's aunts, Julia and Sarah Pattle, had married men who had risen high in the service of our Government in India. My great uncles, Charles Hay Cameron and Henry Thoby Prinsep, were august, venerable, white-haired invalids, to whose sofas and bedsides I was ceremoniously brought for a few moments' conversation. They stand out clearly in my recollection, not only as noble-looking specimens of the race, but for what my father told me of their wisdom and knowledge and of the part which they had played in the making and administration of law in India. My two great aunts, Julia Cameron and Sarah Prinsep, were every bit as remarkable as their husbands. Each was a woman of devouring and tempestuous activity, who made things happen all round her, Julia the creator of artistic photography and Sarah the well-known hostess of Little Holland House, where you would meet Burne Jones, and George Eliot, and Herbert Spencer and Mr. Gladstone, indeed all the most interesting men and women of the period. It seems to have been a common property of the Pattle sisters to ensnare men of genius in their train. My aunt Julia, who lived during my childhood at Freshwater, claimed the allegiance of Alfred Tennyson and Henry Taylor. My Aunt Sarah for forty-one years provided a home for G. F. Watts. My grandmother's personal pets among the poets were Coventry Patmore and Aubrey de Vere, whose talents were held up to our somewhat sceptical and irreverent minds, as yet altogether unprepared for the message of these exalted mortals, with a sentiment amounting to veneration.

I mention these illustrious beings not because they often came across us, but because the names of poets and artists were often on the lips of our elders, so that I very soon came to think that nothing was finer in the world than art and poetry. How earnestly my sister Florence and I would long to be allowed to sit very quietly in the big studio at Little Holland House where G. F. Watts (the Signor as he was called), all glorious in his black skull-cap, worked at one of those large imaginative canvasses which entranced our elders, and were all the more exciting to us children because the background was painted in by a young German named Conrad, who was actually, as we understood, under sentence of death for having run away to escape military service in Prussia. How romantic and brave of Conrad to be under sentence of death! We admired him almost as much as the Signor himself. So with men and women doing interesting work around us we moved forward into life. The grave and noble Signor, the fantastic Patmore, the beautiful Aubrey de Vere; the tall and majestic figure of Henry Taylor with his long white beard flowing over his scarlet dressing-gown, are figures which float back to me from the past; considerable men,

MRS. HERBERT FISHER
(*from a photograph by Julia Cameron*)

no doubt, in themselves, but magnified by the flattering medium of family worship through which, as children, we were taught to look on them.

The most urgent problem when Aunt Julia was about was how to escape being photographed, for the exposure lasted 120 seconds and was a sore trial to the patience of a child. With Aunt Sarah there were no pitfalls. A garden party at Little Holland House, where there was a boat-swing and ices, and cream with one's tea, and every conceivable amusement which a child could desire, was elysium. Am I overstating the place which Aunt Sarah captured in the imagination of a small child? I think not. Angela Thirkell, in her charming *Three Houses*, has described my impressions. To any who would seek to recapture the magic of those old days at Little Holland House when this great and gracious woman dispensed hospitality to her wide circle of Victorian friends of every age and of every degree of eminence and notoriety I would recommend Mrs. Thirkell's pages. I recover here the half-remembered emotions of my childhood.

My mother was a saint. A more selfless unworldly being never drew breath. Her life was a perpetual surrender of ease and comfort to the service of others. Enjoying like her mother and her two sisters and many other members of her family great personal beauty, she never gave it a thought or was visited even by the faintest suspicion of vanity. She was not and made no pretence to be an intellectual. Of education she had received that measure only which was thought in her own generation to be suitable to young ladies of gentle birth. She never went to school or college, had no classics (save what she taught her children) or science, but two delightful accomplishments she enjoyed. Her colloquial French was perfect and the piano sang under her exquisite touch. I think that the qualities which must have impressed most people about my mother were an ardent rushing inexhaustible benevolence, and a swiftness in words and action in all the affairs of common life which left everyone around her breathless. She was the mother of eleven children, upon each of whom she showered an unforgettable treasury of affection and solicitude. What she endured on our behalf, what anxieties and anxious vigils when we were ill, what tremors of apprehension when we were entering upon any new stage of our careers! No mother can ever have lived more vividly in the lives of all her children. For my mother the family was everything. She had no time or inclination for public causes. She was tortured by no intellectual doubts. A simple religious faith sustained her in an atmosphere where everything was put in question. The five things most precious in a woman, family love, faith in goodness, music and poetry, high courage in misfortune were all hers. She was my first teacher and my best. I still recall the eager animation of her little classes held round the nursery table. Delight in learning came to me from her. She seemed to be finding out things for the first time with us. With her the lesson was an exciting adventure, not a gloomy task. 'She was content', as De Quincey wrote of Dorothy Wordsworth, 'to be ignorant in many things, but what she knew and had really mastered lay where it could not be disturbed, in the temple of her own most fervid heart.'

My Boyhood

MY father's promotion from a Court appointment to a Judgeship in Cornwall released us from our London bondage. To the unspeakable delight of the older children the household moved to the Sussex coast, and here at Blatchington Court, near Seaford, in full view of the sea and the Downs, we spent four happy years riding and bathing, hunting with the Southdowns, and birds-nesting or wandering over the lovely Down country which spread northwards and eastwards to Firle and Eastbourne. The family exchequer was far from being ample, but in those days of light taxation a modest income went a long way, and since my parents were prepared to spend their all upon the children the best kind of English country life was within our reach.

Seaford was one of the Cinque Ports, a fact of which we were promptly informed, but which was less impressive in the nursery than the dark report of our little village of Blatchington in the days of smuggling. I still remember the awe with which we looked upon a bronzed villager of the name of Green who was said to have smuggled as a boy. Green, who wore ear-rings, was one of my early heroes. He had all the marks of a man of action. One day climbing down the chalk face of Seaford Head he robbed the nest of the Peregrine falcon, and enriched my collection with two precious eggs.

The memory of those Blatchington days is now very

dim, but little odds and ends recur to my mind as I
endeavour to recall that distant period of my life. I
remember at the age of eight writing a play in blank verse
with lyrical choruses on the subject of Orestes. I remember reading *Old Mortality* again and again. I remember
how my ambition to grow up like Green the smuggler
was replaced by my intention to rival Sir Walter Scott.
I remember how on Christmas Eve we used to gather
in the Hall to watch the Mummers play *St. George and
the Dragon*; how excited we used to feel by the annual
Lewes riots on Guy Fawkes' day, how we kept two tame
ravens who ultimately disgraced themselves by pecking
a hole in a neighbour's donkey, and how I missed the
best part of the best run of the season by an ignominious
fall on Firle Beacon. More particularly do I remember
the figs, the mulberries, and pears in the garden, and
the attempts of the whole family to instruct Coventry
Patmore the poet in the national game of cricket.

Coventry Patmore was one of our rare visitors; for
the drawback attaching to my father's removal to the
country was that he lost touch with a wide and interesting circle of London friends, and that the precious capital
of these long friendships was accordingly lost to the
family. Most particularly do I now regret that among
these earlier friends Rossetti and Matthew Arnold were
never known to us.

The business of the Vice-Warden of the Stannaries
was, owing to the decline of the Cornish tin trade, so
much less exacting than it had once been that the main

part of it could be dispatched in four sessions of a fortnight each at Truro. On these Cornish voyages my father
would now and again take me as his companion, and when
this happened, always to my great content, we generally
managed to combine a few days' pleasure with business,
travelling from Helston to the Lizard for a breath of sea
air, or else staying at St. Ives with the Leslie Stephens
in the circle of beautiful children and brilliant intel-
lectuals which is commemorated in my cousin Virginia's
sensitive fantasia 'To the Lighthouse'. Virginia was a
small child then, and was only in her teens when she lost
the lovely mother who was adored by us all and to whom
in this commemorative volume she pays an exquisite
tribute. Her father Leslie, so formidable within the
home, was a different creature when he was striding
over the Cornish cliffs, botanizing as he went, repeating
poetry, and overflowing with good spirits and enjoyment.
I learnt to know him from these St. Ives visits and always
held him in deep affection and regard. Another image
comes back to me. The sea round the Cornish coast was
a revelation. Nothing which I had seen from the Sussex
or Devon shore had prepared me for the magical
translucency of those greens and blues. The raptures of
a schoolboy are naturally constrained, but they are real
and live in the remembrance.

In 1878, the year of my going to Winchester, my
father inherited from an aunt a house in the New Forest,
and with great reluctance, for he loved the South Downs
and was ill-pleased by the pedestrian architecture of his

new acquisition ('unfit for a gentleman to live in'), removed us to Whitley Ridge, near Brockenhurst. At first we shared the deep dejection of our parents. We should lose the sea. We should lose the beautiful galloping ground behind our house. We should lose the mulberry-tree, the fig-trees, and the spinney which was so full of birds' nests, and the Hove cricket ground where we used to be taken to watch the heroes of the Sussex Eleven, and our circle of village friends to whom we had become greatly attached and all for a dreadful vulgar house in the New Forest. The prospect was one which filled us all with melancholy foreboding.

In point of fact the New Forest was a paradise for children. In one respect only was it disappointing. There was a great deal less bird life than we were accustomed to, and for such an eager bird-lover as I was at that stage of my existence this was dashing to the spirits. In all other respects, however, the Forest proved to be an incomparable playground for a large growing family of children. At every season, in any mood, it was a source of perpetual joy. The insufficiency of our house was soon forgotten in the glories of the country in which it stood. As my father was fond of hunting and was a good horseman, his sons, so long as we were established in the New Forest, had all the riding which they could desire.

Well do I remember the leave-out days from Winchester when my brother Arthur and I used to rush down to Brockenhurst by an early train to find my father waiting for us at the station with the carriage, the drive home, my mother at the door, the gigantic breakfast, and then the merry start to the meet, the gallop with the New Forest hounds and the high tea in the evening, before the hour came round for the train back to school.

Since during the winter and spring holidays we could only expect to hunt three days a fortnight we were taught all the little ways by which the strength of our horses could be husbanded. To dismount at every possible opportunity at the covert side, or again during a great part of the journey home, when we would trudge mile after mile on foot leading our horses, and to see to it that our mounts were properly fed and watered and rubbed down at the end of the day before we left the stables; these were precepts which we were trained to observe. It was also a very particular part of my father's philosophy that however muddy might be the weather, no son of his should appear at the meet showing a speck of mud on his boots. I still vividly remember the care with which we were instructed to negotiate the puddles in the way, and my father's agony of mind when through inattention or lack of skill we splashed ourselves during the ride to the august ceremony of the meet. All this was very solemn and important for us at that stage of our existence, and, I am convinced, very good discipline.

To the fashionable hunting man, accustomed to ride with the Quorn and the Pytchley, a day with the New Forest Hounds must seem a very tame affair. There are no grass fields, no fences. There is much boggy land, a good deal of slow intricate woodland hunting, a good deal of pounding up and down muddy rides in the enclosures, before the fox can be coaxed into the open, and often a day without anything which can be reasonably described as a good run. Yet to anyone who cares about nature and the peculiar characteristics of the English countryside, this slow hunting in beautiful country, much of it wooded, but much of it open moorland, hunting so slow that no countryman on his shaggy little Forest pony need despair of seeing a great deal of the fun, especially if, as most country men do, he knows the lie of the land, is delightful. Specially enjoyable was the Hunt in April (for in the Forest we reckoned to kill a May fox) when the days were lengthening out and the going was dry and the young leaves were on the trees, and when, dawdling about pleasantly in the sunshine during the early hours of the afternoon, we would start a fox about tea-time and gallop to our hearts' desire through the long evening light, returning home happy and tired for a late supper after nightfall.

In those days before the motor-car hunting in the New Forest was the enjoyment of a comparatively small circle of Forest residents, known to one another and familiar with the country. There was George Meyrick, from Hinton Admiral, the good-natured slow-witted master of the Foxhounds, and Francis Lovell of Hinchelsea, the tall handsome one-armed Crimean veteran, who with two hard-riding daughters hunted the staghounds (a perfect horseman who went about his work in silent concentration as if the destinies of the world rested on his shoulders), and Gerald Lascelles the fashionable verderer, and old Major Martin Powell of Lyndhurst whose bookshelves were filled with top boots, and a score of other wholesome happy cheery sportsmen whose open-air figures are pleasant to recall. But to this company of familiar followers of the hunt there was one day added a stranger to the Forest, a substantial old gentleman with a grey beard, quietly but excellently attired and mounted on a well-groomed grey horse. From that day forward Mr. Mudge, for that was his name, became of all followers of the hunt the most faithful. Yet he remained the darkest mystery. That he was a townsman seemed certain, that he was retired from a city bank was freely rumoured. Living a solitary bachelor life in a little house in Brockenhurst, Mr. Mudge knew nobody, and save for the conventional greetings on the hunting field spoke to nobody. No one saw Mr. Mudge in church or at a garden party or at a cricket match or indeed anywhere in the summer, but with November Mr. Mudge returned to life. Season after season this quiet little old gentleman would be found taking his pleasure by the covert side on his iron grey, and getting out of that carefully husbanded steed as much health and happiness as a modest old man in his retirement may hope to enjoy.

To the finest moral natures blood sports will always be repellent. There is no real answer to Wordsworth's

> Never to take your pleasure or your joy
> From sorrow of the meanest thing that breathes,

but as human nature is in fact constituted, hunting is a more wholesome form of occupying the spare hours of country folk than many other modes of amusement which in default of hunting would be resorted to. Mr. Mudge, that retiring inexpressive devotee of the chase, suffered, I venture to submit, no evil from the sport of hunting and the leisurely open-air companionship of the hunt, and since it was by no means part of his pleasure or practice to be in at the death can have seen very little of blood.

Brockenhurst Park was at the time owned by John Morant, a man of most rigid Tory principles who regretted the abolition of slavery (for his fortune was derived from Jamaica) and regarded Sir Robert Peel as the greatest traitor in English history. But Morant, a delicate little man of fastidious manners, was very far from being the commonplace Tory squire. He hated field sports, he disliked rural companionship, he had no interest in farming, he disapproved of public schools, he took no part in local affairs. Music was his only passion. He played the organ himself and would gather professionals around him on the Sunday for little private concerts to which no one in the neighbourhood was invited. My mother's charming touch on the piano and my sister Florence's brilliant violin were welcome additions of strength to these musical Sundays. And as the three Morant children were roughly of like age to ourselves the association between the two families was close and happy. A beautiful Park was added to our

E

playground. The sumptuous gardens which had only
been rendered possible by the labour of Jamaican slaves,
were, so far as the constant enjoyment of them was concerned, almost as good as our own.

Among the poets Tennyson was our family god. I
have never unlearned or attempted to unlearn my boyish
admiration of him. I still think him the most musical
of our poets and the greatest master of our poetic
English language since Shakespeare. Yet I am conscious
that, since many of the conditions which gave him a
supreme hold upon the affections of his generation have
now passed away, it is impossible that he should ever
recapture his lost empire. It is a proud memory that I
was once privileged as a small schoolboy to take a walk
with the old poet at Faringford. I remember how he
came sweeping along in his picturesque slouch hat and
long cloak, how as I trotted by his side he recited or
intoned choice passages from his poetry, how from time
to time he would turn round to me with a childish satis-
faction and say, 'Isn't that grand?', and how keenly,
despite his near sight, he would descry beauty in a
flower and bring it to the notice of his companion. All
poets no doubt have their off moments when they
descend from Parnassus, and think the ordinary thoughts
of ordinary mortals. But with Tennyson I imagine that
these moments of relaxation were fewer than with most,
and that he sustained himself for long periods with
effortless ease in the rarefied atmosphere of poesy. At
any rate the companionship of a dull little Winchester

schoolboy was not enough to bring him down to earth. He was, no doubt, spoiled by admiring ladies. My old great-aunt, Julia Cameron, who was a close neighbour at Freshwater, was a sinner in that respect and one of his most inveterate adorers, though she did not scruple to scold him when he deserved it. But no spoiling could rob Tennyson of his essential greatness and simplicity. In some respects he had retained more of that rough county Lincolnshire than one would gather from his son's filial tribute. He liked strong language and strong drink. Nor do I forget that I was privileged to witness the preparation for the poet's weekly bath, the round shallow tub on the landing, and the tall cans of hot water which it was the office of the coachman to pour over the stalwart frame of the seated Laureate.

As I write these lines I ask myself whether the sunny carefree existence which we enjoyed in our New Forest home during the eighties and nineties of the last century would be equally possible to-day. The idea of a European war in which our country would be involved never entered our minds. Even the arena of national politics seemed dimly remote. Save for Auberon Herbert who from time to time descended upon us from his hermitage at Burley we saw no politicians, and Auberon Herbert, the most enchanting of visionaries, who preached against state interference in all its forms, even in taxation, was a thousand miles away from the practical realities of life. Though we noted and deplored the wretched cottages on a neighbour's estate, the social problem did not torment us. Of European history, which should be a cardinal study in every household, we knew nothing, and only the appearance of Seeley's *Making of England* brought home to me at the end of my Winchester career the true character of our Empire. At the present day boys and girls in their 'teens tear life's problems to tatters. We were content to leave those grave concerns to our elders. Against a background of hunting and dancing in the winter, of cricket and tennis in the summer, with always a good deal of home-made music, the boys of the family trod the narrow way which was supposed to lead to scholastic success. Until I married I had never entered the House of Commons. The only shadow which darkened the smooth surface of our Forest holidays was the knowledge that each one of us had to make his own way in life. A certain nervousness at this point, emanating from my father, percolated to his offspring. Only our wonderful mother possessed a confident serenity. She knew that her girls would marry and that her boys would make good. Through her skill and devotion four daughters and seven sons survived into middle life. Of the family of eleven which at Brockenhurst lived together under the same roof, two sons and three daughters still survive. Our paths in life diverged widely. But at rare intervals and then always with intense enjoyment do we renew the family companionship, and Adam Smith's generalization that men are differentiated more by the nature of their calling than by any other single fact is, I think, sub-

MR. HERBERT FISHER

(*from a portrait by G. F. Watts*)

stantiated in our case. *Studia abeunt in mores*. Each separate mode of life has left its distinct mark. Yet I suspect that if fate had so ordered, our roles might have been exchanged and that the kind of work which each one of us has been set to do by the chances of fate might have been accomplished, not perhaps so well, but not without credit, by the others.

Two of my younger brothers ultimately rose to eminence in their respective callings. William, the sailor, directed the Anti-Submarine department in the Great War, rose to be Commander-in-Chief of the Mediterranean Fleet, and but for his premature death at the age of sixty-two would have been First Sea Lord. Edwin, the youngest of the family, is Chairman of Barclay's Bank and a figure in the City. Two other brothers were cut short by the War in mid career before they had an opportunity of developing their remarkable gifts. Edmund was a naturalist, a sportsman, and an architect. He had an extraordinary sympathy with animals, a virtuoso's discernment of porcelain and painting, and a rare and individual taste in the exercise of his profession. The Hall of Somerville College, Oxford, and the Protestant Church in Rome were among his most important buildings. He died for his country. Though he was the father of seven children and well over military age, he volunteered for military service, received a Commission, and succumbed to a malady contracted in the trenches after the exertions of the battle of Cambrai. Charles went down in H.M.S. *Invincible*, in the Battle of Jutland. He too volunteered for military or naval service when much over age. A widely beloved Oxford don, a distinguished Latinist, and an Oxford and Sussex cricketer, Charles was an outstanding figure in his generation. His magnificent physique, and fine intellectual head, his rich hearty laugh and keen sense of humour, gave him a natural ascendancy in any company. When he and William were together, as they often were, they filled the room with a sense of their presence. Both were born leaders of men. Each was the centre of a wide circle of devoted and admiring friends. Two poets have recalled their admiration of Charles, Robert Bridges by his dedication of the 'Spirit of Man', and J. S. Phillimore in one of the finest English elegies. As for William his epitaph is the defeat of the U-Boat campaign.

The brother nearest to me in age was likewise one of the martyrs of our Imperial wars. Arthur was a professional soldier. He went from Winchester and Christ Church into the army, and for almost the whole of his short life was far away from home, in India, in the Sudan, in Uganda, and in South Africa. A shy, tender, sensitive fellow, he seemed ill-fitted for the life of a serving soldier under scorching sun. In the South African War his constitution, already enfeebled by blackwater fever, broke down under the strain. His name may be read in the South African Gateway at Winchester.

My eldest sister Florence had, I am disposed to think, an element of genius. Certainly she was unlike other people, more perceptive and with a peculiar strain of wayward originality. Very beautiful, but utterly devoid of personal vanity, she was in girlhood possessed by a passion for the violin, practising her. art with a severe concentration and attaining to a high amateur standard, and these artistic accomplishments were combined in her with a devotion to animals extreme to the point of fantasy. She used to say, and I do not think lightly, that she preferred animals to humans. When she was a girl at Brockenhurst there was Moses her favourite dog; later a long procession of dogs, cats, monkeys, foxes, moles, meerkats, mongooses, bush cats, and marmosets, accompanied by a variety of birds, passed through her house. I remember hearing that she took one of her daughters out to a ball bearing in her arms a tray of recently hatched thrushes which she was bringing up by hand and was not prepared to leave out of her sight. Her first husband was that wonderful historical scholar, F. W. Maitland, whom she nursed with great devotion through long years of illness until his death in 1906; her second, Sir Francis Darwin, the distinguished botanist to whom she was married some years later. Her interests, however, were neither historical nor scientific, but in the spheres of music, poetry, and drama, and in the wilder and less conventional sides of human nature. If birds and cats had the first call upon her affections country folk were preferred to townsfolk, and gypsies and wanderers of all kinds to sedentary villagers. Though she was fond of scribbling humorous and fantastic plays and novelettes for family consumption she gave nothing to the world in her lifetime. But after her death on March 5th, 1920, six of her country plays written during the last eleven years at Brookthorpe, her Gloucestershire home, were published by Cecil Sharp. Her plays, which have been much acted by country folk to country audiences, display great insight into the working of the peasant mind, and one of them, entitled *The New Year*, is a tragedy of rare beauty and power.

The other family genius by general consent was my fourth brother Hervey, who displayed, despite the cruel ill health which prevented him from going to school or entering a profession, Johnsonian powers of intellect and raillery. Hervey, who without formal education of any kind outdistanced all competitors for the Brackenbury scholarship at Balliol, while he had obvious gifts for history and literature was first and foremost a metaphysician. That he would have been in the first rank of English philosophers had he kept his health I have little doubt. But he was allowed to fall by a nurse when a baby, and suffered from tubercular trouble in the spine leading to a long series of unavailing operations which only temporarily mitigated his discomfort and pain. His long illness, which culminated in a serious but temporary mental breakdown, after which his physical health improved, cast a shadow over our family life. My mother, and after her death my sister Adeline Vaughan Williams, spent their lives in his sick-room, and his illness was the cause of our giving up our house in the

New Forest for Brighton, a town in which we had no friends and where my father was forced at an advanced age to seek for new and less congenial occupations.

An invalid in a family is an education in charity. Not that it entailed any great measure of self-sacrifice to sit by the bedside of an invalid so wise, witty, and amusing as, save in moments of exceptional pain, Hervey could be relied on to be. He was everyone's favourite and the best company in the world. I have always regarded it as a tragedy that so robust and independent a mind should have been prevented by a physical accident from making its contribution to the life of the country.

F

My Schooldays

Of all human faculties memory is the most capricious. The experiences of my school life which present themselves most vividly and frequently to my consciousness bear no relation whatever to any scale of established values. I remember trifles, I forget important things. I remember the enormous feet of the Headmaster at my preparatory school at Maidenhead, the stiff red beard of the mathematical master, and how pleasant it was to pick blackberries for the blackberry-and-apple tart which was served to us on Michaelmas Day after the goose had been disposed of. I remember too the vivid disgust inspired in my mind by the huge piles of stale bread and disagreeable butter which constituted our evening meal, and how we envied the under-master his cottage loaf and boiled egg. Of the teaching I recall nothing. It made no impression; but I am certain that the competition was good for me, helping to shake me out of my early habits of vague musing and to teach me the art of attention and critical reading. When I came home for my first holidays my father, who hardly concealed his contempt for the methods of my pedagogues, was bound to concede that school had put an edge on my mind.

Only one recollection of this institution strikes me as being of any historical interest. Our observance of Sunday was uncommonly strict. No boy was allowed to read a book which had not been passed by the authorities as fit for Sunday reading, and under this rubric all fiction and most literature was taboo. I was the fortunate possessor of a small volume of Lithuanian folk-stories upon which the formidable Headmaster was pleased to smile. This book then I was allowed to read. It was a bleak privilege.

In compensation for this comprehensive abridgement of private reading on Sunday, the Headmaster gathered us together in class and took us through Keble's *Christian Year* at the rate of one poem per week. We were called upon to read these poems aloud and to explain them verse by verse and line by line. I believe that good judges concede to Mr. Keble not only a rare piety of soul, but also a vein of genuine poetry, but I am sure that he is not a poet to put before boys. His fine-drawn Anglican sentiment struck us as being fantastic and remote.

I cannot say that I was ever really happy at my preparatory school. Indeed I vividly remember thinking during my first term that all joys were at an end and that I should never know what happiness was again. Long years of exile among hostile aliens seemed to stretch before me. At times I thought that life was utterly odious, for I was tall, awkward, rather dreamy, not especially good at games, and dressed in a Norfolk jacket, which put me beyond the pale. A welcome attack of whooping-cough shortened the miseries of my first term, and not very long afterwards I returned home to prepare for a scholarship at Winchester.

After Maidenhead Winchester was paradise. Here was true liberty, here were sausages for breakfast, here was the proud power of supplementing the evening tea with 'cargoes' as we called them of provisions from home.

I did not succeed in winning a scholarship and, indeed, owing to a sunstroke was unable to complete the examination. Perhaps this was as well, for College boys were expected to work harder than Commoners, and being somewhat overgrown I stood in need of a fallow time. Besides it was my good fortune to be under the best of Housemasters and in the best of Houses.

When I first went to Winchester the most distinguished boy in my House was Edward Grey, later Viscount Grey of Fallodon. I was Grey's fag and found him the kindest of masters. He had the reputation of being an excellent scholar, able to get a school prize if he cared to exert himself; but he was not set on academical honours, and the pleasures of a solitary afternoon on the Itchen with a rod far outweighed possible, indeed almost certain, triumphs on the cricket-field.

Among the senior boys in the school was Frederic Kenyon (later Principal Librarian of the British Museum), George Talbot (later a Puisne Judge), and L. A. Selby Bigge, who was for so many years a tower of strength to the Board of Education. These, however, were gods of the Empyrean. A humble junior could only admire them at a distance. Of the boys nearer me in age the most remarkable was, I think, Lionel Johnson, whose acquisitions in English literature were even at that early period of his life truly remarkable. He was a diminutive, ethereal creature, with a pallid beautiful face, an omnivorous reader, quite remote from the ordinary interests of the school and indeed contemptuous of them, but passionately enamoured of the beauties of Winchester. A certain aura surrounded him for he was reputed to be a Buddhist, to have read all the books in the school library, and to drink eau de cologne for his amusement.

I enjoyed every moment of my life at Winchester; the work, the games, the society of my fellows and of the masters, and the compelling beauty of the old buildings, of the College Meads, and of the sweet water-meadows among which the College is set, were all delightful. The teaching was picturesquely irregular, some of it most brilliant and inspiring, some quite inefficient. I well remember my first hour 'up to books' or in class. The master, or don as we called him, though a fine classical scholar, was notoriously incapable of preserving discipline. Two boys were playing fives at one end of the room; one boy was sawing away the leg of the master's table; the remainder were yelling as loud as their lungs would permit. Everyone was in the best of humour. It was pandemonium.

The part of the Winchester system which I particularly enjoyed was the Greek and Latin composition. The division master would set two long 'tasks' in prose and verse; a fine piece of Shakespeare, for instance, for Greek iambics or a sonnet from Wordsworth for Latin elegiacs, and these exercises were to be done in a boy's free time during the week. I took an immense pleasure in committing my English poetry or prose, as the case might be, to memory and in turning over possible renderings in Greek or Latin on country walks or in spare moments of the working day. I am sure that there could have been no finer education in literary taste. Before I left Winchester I think that I had rendered most of the finest speeches in Shakespeare into Greek or Latin.

On the other hand, the method of taking us through our classical texts was bad; for it was so minutely grammatical that very little ground was covered. I do not refuse merits to this minute and careful handling of classical texts, but it should be intermingled with encouragement to read the classics for aesthetic enjoyment and the interest of the subject-matter as well. Unfortunately very few of us realized that our Headmaster expected us to supplement the vigorous drill in textual and grammatical criticism which we received in the classroom with general reading on our own account.

Two great events of the school year were the annual cricket match with Eton and the contests at football between the three sections of the School known as College, House, and Commoners. Though I was only a Second Eleven cricketer I was as much excited as anybody else about Eton matches, and before the Great War could have recalled all the important scores and many of the unimportant ones made in these great encounters during my school life. But my memory is failing me. I have recently been convicted of a failure to recall the issue of an important six game at football in which I played myself as 'Last Behind'. Such a lapse fifteen years ago would have seemed to me incredible, and a signal mark of intellectual decay.

In their different ways Ridding, Fearon, and Edmund Morshead, the three principal classical masters when I came to Winchester, were hard to surpass. Ridding, besides being a far-sighted organizer, was a classical scholar with a fine gift for composition; Fearon, less eminent as a man and a scholar, was incomparable as a teacher of history to boys, while Edmund Morshead brought to his work a range of knowledge in modern and ancient literature, and what is more important a poet's enthusiasm for beautiful things which for many of us who came under his influence were sources of unending delight.

There were other excellent masters besides these three, one of whom, A. K. Cook, the historian of Winchester College, is still happily alive and flourishing.

Though I belonged to the Debating Society and spoke on the Liberal side (defending, for instance, the Ilbert Bill), I do not think that politics occupied much of my mind as a schoolboy. I was far more interested in poetry. It was, however, at Winchester that I first tried my hand at journalism. There was a school paper known as *The Wykehamist* which some of us voted very dull. We determined to launch a counterblast to be entitled the *Trusty Servant*, and to our huge relief actually cleared seven shillings on the first issue. In time, however, we overstepped the bounds. Authority frowned on us, the paper perished, and I passed on to edit *The Wykehamist*, very much as the Radical member of Parliament becomes by insensible gradations a Tory Peer.

On Saints' Days we were given a whole holiday, and those of us who were fortunate enough to have relations or friends to receive them were given 'leave out'. Nothing can exceed the joy of those leave-out days. My brother Arthur and I would slip off by an early train to our home in the New Forest and spend the day scampering about on our ponies, and if the hounds were anywhere in the neighbourhood we were pretty certain to follow them. The Michaelmas term was rich in these delightful excursions.

Looking back I recognize that our intellectual training was too one-sided. We hardly touched the skirt of the sciences. The vast field of modern knowledge was a closed book to us; but we learned to enjoy the beauties of literature, and those of us who had any turn for history or for exact classical scholarship found every opportunity for exercising and improving those gifts.

Oxford

OXFORD had been my destiny from the first, and among Oxford Colleges family tradition and my father's strong preference pointed to Christ Church. To Christ Church then I should have gone, as my brother Charles went later, but for the special tie linking Winchester to New College which was brought to my father's notice by the Winchester authorities. Since New College offered every year six Scholarships to Winchester boys, it was considered a point of honour at Winchester to reserve of her best for New College. My father yielded with a sigh to the 'gentleman's agreement'. I was in due course entered for a Winchester scholarship, and was elected Head of the Roll, so much to my surprise that when the Warden's butler brought me, according to custom, the New College telegram announcing the list I was hard put to it to raise the sovereign with which this service was by tradition remunerated.

Dr. Sewell, the Warden of New College, was a 'gremial' Wykehamist. He had entered Winchester as a small boy and in due course proceeded to be a Scholar, a Fellow, and subsequently Bursar and Warden of New College. All his life had been spent in the Wykehamical atmosphere, all his care was to preserve the Wykehamical tradition. He had been elected to the comfortable emoluments of a Life Fellowship on an examination conducted by the Fellows of the College which on the classical side involved a translation from a single chapter of history, on the mathematical an explanation of the fifth proposition of the first book of Euclid. He was not, then, a learned man or even the friend of good letters. Indeed, he gave it as his opinion that most of the trouble in the world came from the writing of books and that it would be better for us all if no books were written. He did not teach, he did not lecture, he did not publish, he rarely admonished. Yet it must not be supposed that the Warden was indolent. On the routine affairs of the College, including its relation with the University, he bestowed a minute and affectionate diligence, and the muniments of the College contain proofs of his antiquarian zeal and of the clear and delicate handwriting which remained with him to the end.

Dr. Sewell was already a venerable figure when I arrived as a freshman in October 1884. 'The most important part of your education here, Mr. Fisher', he observed to me on the evening of my first Sunday, 'will be the reading of the lessons in Chapel.' Yet to that education the Warden failed to contribute more than an injunction that one should be counted for a comma, two for a semi-colon, three for a colon, and four for a full stop.

Of the older studies of the University he knew little. The newer studies were altogether beyond his ken. He was a survivor from that earlier age when New College, being confined to Wykehamists of the Anglican Church and debarred by privilege from taking university examinations, was at once contracted, indolent, orthodox, and obscure. It is very much to the credit of the Warden's goodness that although a strong conservative by nature, he adapted himself to the changing spirit of the age and accepted without demur the valuable and numerous alterations which converted a medieval little Wykehamical seminary into a large Oxford college of the modern type.

Since it was the habit of the Warden to invite every freshman to breakfast during his first term, when after the first frost was broken his charming old-fashioned courtesy delighted us all; and since at the end of term we were bidden to shake hands with him at Collections, and had further the opportunity of seeing him in Chapel and Hall, we were in a distant way aware of his presence among us. His age, his gentle affability, his trim appearance, his punctual discharge of conventional duty, made him a respectable figure. He was popularly known as the Shirt and regarded by his juniors with a kind of affectionate condescension.

Later, when I was a Fellow of the College, I knew more of him. Never was he happier than when, accompanied by Mr. Wickham, the Steward of the College manors, and by one of the Fellows as outrider, he carried out his annual Progress round the College estates. Then the Oxfordshire rustic might behold a little old clerical gentleman with a tall silk hat and white bands driving in a carriage and pair with two young gentlemen, his eyes shielded by an antique pair of spectacles bought at the time of the first railway train, and in his hand a little black bag from which he would extract a looking-glass and a comb in order that his grey locks, of which he was careful, might be at their best when confronted with the feminine charms of the farmhouse. The Warden was delighted with these excursions, which then occupied a great part of July. He knew the farmers, their wives and families, asked after the fruit-trees and flowers, and was ready with shrewd comment on the crops. On the subject of remission of rent or other concessions, he was as stiff as a ramrod. When a particularly ingratiating farmer's wife asked for help towards disinfecting some rooms after two cases of typhoid in her family, my venerable friend replied sternly, and to the lady's obvious amusement, 'It is you, Madam, who should compensate the College for allowing its premises to get into such an insanitary condition.'

The Warden still goes on Progress, but the Manor Courts are no longer held. No longer does the College bailiff read out the opening proclamation, 'Oyez, oyez, all ye who owe suit and service to the Warden and Scholars of St. Mary's College, Oxford', or administer the oath to the Homage of the Manor, or when the labours of the Court have been completed reward the Homage with a gold sovereign to be instantly converted into liquid refreshment at the nearest pub. The ancient tenures were swept away under the terms of the great Act for the reform of Real Property Law which was introduced to the House of Commons by my old friend Leslie Scott, a New College man, when he was Solicitor-

AT OXFORD
(as an undergraduate)

AT WINCHESTER

General in Mr. Lloyd George's Second Coalition Government. As I sat on the Treasury Bench listening to the learned Solicitor's Second Reading speech, my thoughts wandered to these quaint vestiges of medieval English rural life which I had been privileged to enjoy when acting as outrider to Warden Sewell, and which were then fast passing away under the hammer blows of my friend's stentorian eloquence.

My undergraduate years at Oxford were not among the happiest of my life. Apart from a strained heart, a legacy from Winchester football, a severe attack of jaundice very largely wrecked my first term. The Oxford climate did not appear to suit me, and I felt slightly out of sorts during much of the time. Nor could the eldest son of a large family, not too well provided for, shake off a sense of anxiety as to his future. The Schools would be important, perhaps vital, and these wretched examinations spread a cloud over the landscape. As for my undergraduate career it was not in any way distinguished. The bright particular star of my year was Gilbert Murray who swept off all the classical prizes. Beside his glittering achievements mine were modest indeed. Perhaps my greatest claim to distinction was that in the October following my Final Schools I was elected on examination with Murray to a Prize Fellowship in Classics at New College.

Of my tutors at New College two still survive—P. E. Matheson and D. S. Margoliouth.[1] I will say nothing

[1] Professor Margoliouth died in March 1940.

save that no young man could come under either of
them without deriving benefit from the love of literature
and learning which they manifested in their teaching
and in their lives. Margoliouth was rightly regarded by
us all as a prodigy of linguistic acquisition. Few men
can know more words than he, and if any sense of com-
placency existed in the minds of the New College scholars
it was very soon dispersed after an hour with such a
master of tongues, and yet Greek and Latin were the
least of his accomplishments. Even as a young man he
was at home in Hebrew, Syriac, Arabic, and Persian.
Such zeal was infectious. The wide span of his intellectual interests stimulated our energies. Under his
inspiration I read Persian for a term with my friend,
E. D. MacLagan, who was going out to India. These
studies, alas! were not continued, but it was perhaps
profitable to a future historian that they should have
begun.

The biggest figure in College and also in the affairs of
the University was Alfred Robinson. So worldly wise
and eloquent, so statesmanlike and weighty did he appear
to be, that we undergraduates felt no political honours, had
he aspired to a public career, would have been beyond his
reach. In reality, however, as his premature death was
to show, he had not the physical stamina for the House
of Commons. But as an academic statesman he towered
above his contemporaries. The University and College
owe him much. He was one of the makers of the inter-
collegiate lecture system and of the larger New College.

His lectures on Logic and Aristotle's *Politics* filled the College Hall. A strong substantial common sense made him the best of critics, and perhaps to the ordinary undergraduate he was the more helpful by reason of the fact that he was primarily not a scholar but a disinterested man of the world.

A happily contrasted character was that of my other Greats tutor, W. L. Courtney, the most versatile of men, scholar, philosopher, dramatist, journalist, rowing enthusiast, the author of innumerable books, and during the later half of his life widely known as Editor of the *Daily Telegraph* and of the *Fortnightly Review*. Robinson, venerable, stately, grey-bearded, was the incarnation of mild sagacity. Courtney, young, energetic, handsome, with something of the air of a dashing cavalry officer about him, seemed to be designed for the active rather than the speculative life. In truth, though he had a genuine interest in philosophical speculation and no little critical power, he was not by nature a metaphysician. 'Cheerfulness would keep breaking in' as with Mr. Edwards in Boswell's *Johnson*. His lectures and teaching were clear, methodical, and admirably adapted to the purpose which he most successfully achieved of filling the First Class in Literae Humaniores with New College men. I owe him a debt of gratitude for his valuable help. He was a most practical and effective philosophical coach. But his temperament was that of the worldly man of letters rather than of the true thinker. His philosophical writings were slight in texture and his Oxford critics who, on beholding a man so various, described him as a brilliant dilettante, were not far wrong. In effect his spiritual home was not Oxford but the Garrick Club. That he was not altogether at ease in an academic atmosphere was, I think, indistinctly felt by his pupils. Indeed it was one of his sayings, apropos of his colleague W. A. Spooner, that it required a man of genius to live his life in Oxford and that Spooner was a man of genius. To this admirable man, who has achieved immortality by giving his name to a common human failing, a life of pleasant pastoral activity among young men provided an ideal frame. An Oxford college was just the right size for Spooner, and Spooner was just the right size for an Oxford college. His sweet temper, keen wit, and ingratiating appearance, all rose and silver, his capacity for dealing humorously with youthful folly, his sanity and Christian charity, and the perennial freshness of his interests and conversation, made him the most valuable kind of member in a juvenile society such as ours. Men smiled at him, for he was the subject of endless jests, and loved him. His eyesight, which was so imperfect that he could only read with the aid of powerful glasses, debarred him from making any serious addition to knowledge, for his editions of the Histories of Tacitus and of Butler's *Analogy* are unimportant, but nevertheless he was able, despite his grave physical infirmity, not only to teach and examine over a wide field of knowledge but also to keep up an immense correspondence with undergraduates all over the world. Such was his deserved popularity that he was chosen on Dr. Sewell's death without opposition to succeed to the Wardenship. We scholars were bidden to attend his lectures on Aristotle's *Ethics*, a slow deliberate commentary which for indolent and backward men with little knowledge of Greek was just the thing, but as Dean of Divinity, responsible for admonishing undergraduates for failure to attend the compulsory Sunday Chapel, he was brought into contact not with Greats men only but with every member of the College. His engaging manners at these brief interviews were much appreciated by the victims. He seemed to us all to be the happiest and most fortunate man, happy in his charming wife and family, happy in his College drudgery, and above all happy in his opportunities of gentle influence among the young.

This particular type of Oxford Don is not now so common as it was in the eighties. Examinations have become more specialized, teaching and lecturing more erudite. When I was an undergraduate a First Class man in the School of Literae Humaniores was expected to reach a first-class level both in philosophy and history. Now excellence in one of these branches is thought to be sufficient. The prodigious inrush of new knowledge on the side of Greek and Roman antiquities has led to a great deal of work which is really post-graduate being undertaken at the undergraduate stage. The exact distribution of proto-Corinthian pottery engages the mind yet virgin of political knowledge. The Greats man

H

passes from specialist to specialist. Able and enthusiastic tutors pour into him the results of their independent researches. He reads essays to a Greek historian in one term, to a Roman historian in another, to a metaphysician in a third, to a political philosopher in a fourth. The tutor who was prepared, like W. A. Spooner, to teach all these subjects up to a moderate level is a thing of the past.

Hegel, as interpreted by T. H. Green and Caird, was the reigning philosopher in my undergraduate days. It was the fashion among all our instructors to pull J. S. Mill to pieces and consign Herbert Spencer to the nethermost pit. My own Philistine proclivities led me to think more highly both of Mill and of Spencer than my tutors would have approved, but I succeeded in catching the Hegelian phraseology and was prepared to reproduce it in examinations. Moreover, there was one book, inspired by Hegel, to which we were introduced from the first and which made a deep impression on my mind. T. H. Green died in 1883, but his powerful influence survived. His *Prolegomena to Ethics* served as introduction to morals ; a rich, earnest, difficult book, basing the State on Will, and, by its generous interpretation of contractual obligations affording as it seemed to us an impregnable moral foundation for such legislation as Mr. Gladstone's Irish Land Act, which was one of the most hotly controversial measures of that time.

Of that Irish question which was destined to enter so largely into the lives of my political contemporaries I had as an undergraduate but an imperfect conception.

Irish history was known to me, but in the barest outline. I came of an unpolitical family. My father was a Liberal Unionist, so too were Leslie Stephen, my uncle, and F. W. Maitland, my brother-in-law. Nevertheless, having taken the Liberal side as a school-boy and being, I think, to some extent swayed by my friend Gilbert Murray, who felt ardently about the Irish cause, I decided for Home Rule. It was my belief that the Union could not for all time be preserved against the overwhelming sentiment of Catholic Irishmen, and that, as the change was bound to come, the sooner it came the better. That a settlement of the Irish question on Home Rule lines would bring England and America nearer together seemed to me to be a strong argument in favour of the change.

One year of the Oxford Union was sufficient. The debates, save on one memorable occasion when Lord Randolph Churchill was the orator, seemed to me to be wretched, and most unwisely, as I now think, I made no attempt to improve them. The small and select audience of the Palmerston Club, meeting in undergraduates' rooms, was no adequate substitute for the Union as a training ground for public speaking. Oxford then did not give me what, if I had accepted her opportunities, I might have received, the discipline of the public platform. What little I have managed to acquire of the oratorical art was gained from the addresses which I was in the habit of delivering without notes to working-class audiences in Bethnal Green under the kindly encouragement of that most expansive and engaging of Anglican clergymen, Dr. Winnington Ingram, afterwards for many years Bishop of London.

In the University at large Jowett was the most influential academic figure. His reputation as a great Head of a House, as a Platonist, as an inspiring teacher and wise mentor of young men, as a vigorous and innovating Vice-Chancellor, as a master of melodious English prose, and perhaps above all as a Johnsonian character whose shrewd aphorisms passed into general currency, was very high among the senior members of the University, though, among the clever young men of his own College, the bright star had lost some of its earlier brilliance. It was indeed hardly to be expected that after four years of heavy administrative work as Vice-Chancellor he should have kept abreast of the times in scholarship and philosophy. His lectures on the pre-Socratics, though marked by shrewd observations, were desultory; his private teaching was marred by the tendency to settle big controversies by a phrase or an epigram. I remember taking him an essay on Plato's idea of conscience. 'Plato', he pointed out, as I had concluded reading my paper, 'had no idea of conscience', and there the question was left. Yet, though he had passed his prime as a teacher of philosophy, this quaint white-haired, rosy-cheeked little clergyman, who tripped about Oxford in an old-fashioned swallow-tail coat, was still a figure among young men and old. His will was firm, his tongue sharp, his discipline strict. His intellectual courage and sustained devotion to Greek philosophy earned him general respect. In weight of character and in his tonic influence on the lives of younger men he was probably in his own day unequalled. In his mellow old age he was untiring in quiet benevolence. If he sometimes seemed to be unduly worldly, he was perhaps wise in curbing the excessive idealism of youth. For two days he vainly wrestled with me (though I was not of his flock) in the effort to make me take a pleasant holiday tutorship in the house of a distinguished nobleman who could, he thought, help me in my career.

It was only later that I came to know Walter Pater, but he was already (for we had most of us read *Marius the Epicurean*) one of the minor prophets. His ethereal phrases exercised a magical effect. His medium was not that of Jowett, but for young men with aesthetic leanings most seductive. Since he abjured affairs and shrank from teaching, he attracted little notice in the University. Moreover, his personal appearance was most misleading. Who would have suspected that the trim figure with the heavy military moustache, dressed as for Piccadilly, who from time to time emerged from Brasenose, was the archpriest of aesthetic culture? Yet it was in Brasenose that he passed a quasi-hermit existence, distilling the sweetness of his learning and charm to a narrow circle, and pressing with steadfast ardour his literary quest. Others might discuss pupils and examinations and the politics of the hour. Withdrawn into his own private world of beauty, Pater was content that the whirling stream of our vulgar life should pass him by.

Another and more widely famous recluse was the author of *Alice in Wonderland*. Mr. Dodgson (for Lewis Carroll was a pseudonym) was an Anglican clergyman and an ingenious mathematician, to whom, since he was a Student of Christ Church, my father's old College, I was bound by a slender link. To none, however, old or young, did this wayward and original spirit open out its curious treasures. His intense shyness and morbid dislike of publicity made him a figure apart. Only in Common Room, when the port had gone round, and only then on a lucky night, would a tiny drop of fantasy fall from Mr. Dodgson's lips, after which the venerable humorist would resume his tantalizing taciturnity. A dull and steady routine governed the days of this fantastic friend of all the children. Every afternoon he could be seen in his tall silk hat and flowing clerical black striding out to take the air with his inseparable companion the genial and benevolent Vere Bayne, yet another silver-haired Christ Church cleric, upon whose shoulders, equally with Dodgson's, sacerdotal duty lay with a gossamer weight. The old Life Fellowships, often much abused, justified themselves in the case of this admirable pair.

Though Oxford believed much in lecturing, a training in that difficult art, so well understood in Paris, was counted to be unnecessary. Some excellent natural lecturers, such as R. W. Macan in Greek and H. F. Pelham in Roman History, stand out in my recollection. To my regret I never heard R. L. Nettleship on Plato's

Republic, or W. Warde Fowler on Roman antiquities, for they, too, it is clear, were exceptionally gifted in the art of conveying their message to undergraduate audiences. I would not, however, leave the impression that I am ungrateful to my Oxford lecturers. They taught me much. A few hours with Macan or Pelham opened out the vision of a new discipline: that of critically handling the original sources for the history of ancient times. To be taken over the text of Herodotus by Macan, or the epigraphical evidences for the Roman Empire by Pelham, was a fine introduction to the intelligent study of history. We were allowed to catch the secrets of the workshop and shared in the delights of the chase.

Though we did not then know it, we stood on the brink of a brilliant era of archaeological discovery which changed the whole landscape of early Greek history.

Soon after I took my degree my friend and older Wykehamical contemporary, F. G. Kenyon, identified a papyrus in the British Museum as Aristotle's lost treatise on the Athenian constitution. It was the dawn of the age of papyri. In swift succession the literature of Greece was enriched from the treasures of an Egyptian library. The Odes of Bacchylides, the Mimes of Herondas, the Sayings of Jesus, sent a thrill through the world of scholars. And to the new source of fresh knowledge there was added soon afterwards the epoch-making discovery by Arthur Evans of the Minoan civilization of Crete. From that moment onwards archaeological discoveries have descended on us in a cataract which shows no signs of diminishing in volume. Oxford men have taken a prominent, perhaps a leading, part in the great movements of human curiosity, as the names of Kenyon and Evans, of Hogarth, Grenfell and Hunt, of J. L. Myres, Leonard Woolley, J. D. Beazley suffice to remind us. I only mention it because there was a time when I toyed with the idea of devoting myself to the study of Greek antiquity, and was principally impelled to desist from that intention by the belief that nothing important remained to be discovered. Under that belief I parted in the autumn of 1888 with my copy of Muller's *Fragments of the Minor Greek Historians* to Gilbert Murray. Ten years later I might have enrolled myself permanently among the Hellenists.

When I first came to Oxford my own ambition and my father's ambition for me pointed to the Bar and politics. A Prize Fellowship gained soon after my degree seemed to put such a career within my reach, but though my father was willing to have me face the risk, I felt that the family circumstances did not entitle me to do so. Oxford offered an immediate livelihood, and, swallowing worldly ambition, I determined to accept her offer. Yet the path before me was still obscure. My main strength as an undergraduate was thought to lie in philosophy, and for some time after taking my degree I played with the idea, fostered by the offer of a tutorship in philosophy at New College, that I might fit myself to be a metaphysician. Some undergraduates (first among them a brilliant boy named A. C. Taylor) read me their essays on Plato. I delivered a course of lectures on Aristotelian philosophy, read Spinoza's *Ethics* with my friend Harold Joachim, and traded out my superficial acquaintance with the Kantian system. Eventually, however, I came to feel that metaphysics were not my real interest and that a life spent in discussing year by year the same recurrent philosophical problems would prove unsatisfying. F. W. Maitland's advice was decisive. 'No one', he said, 'should teach philosophy at a University unless he either thinks he has it in him to make a system of his own or is zealous to preach the system of another.' The more I reflected upon this advice the wiser it seemed to me to be. And as I felt that I had no vocation either to invent or to preach a philosophical system, I turned my back upon the subject and resolved to devote myself to modern history.

There was at that time, so undergraduates reported, an oracle beyond compare on all matters historical, to be discovered in the Meadow Buildings at Christ Church. He was not a Professor or even a lecturer in Modern History, but he 'knew the stuff'. The undergraduates— a favoured few, for to most men his very existence was unknown—called him 'The Yorker'. His name was Frederick York Powell. He held a lectureship in Law and was reported to be omniscient. He was pointed out to me as he peered into the book-shops in the streets, a burly, bearded, open-air figure dressed in a roomy suit

I

of dark navy blue and, but for his tall hat and pince-nez, looking like a sea captain fresh from his last cruise. To the Yorker I repaired, then, in quest of direction for my projected voyage over the sea of time. His rooms in the Meadow Buildings were one vast disordered litter of books and papers, books of every age, type, and tongue, books against the walls, on the floor, piled high in the bedroom, books about boxing, the trapeze, books in Norse, books on medieval law and countless other subjects, and in the midst of this vast miscellany there was the Yorker—genial, accessible, apparently without a care in the world, and with all his time to give to the chance caller. His advice to me was peculiar and memorable. He pulled out three books from his shelves and said that I should begin my study of modern history with these. They were the *Chanson de Roland*, Maitland's edition of *Bracton's Note Book*, and the *Corpus Poeticum Boreale* ; and then I was taken a tour of this singular library, the reflection of one of the most spacious, sensitive, and versatile intelligences which it has ever been my privilege to meet. A more salutary corrective to the possible danger which I had from the first apprehended, of allowing my view of history to be dominated by examination requirements, could not be conceived. In a quick half-hour I learned an approach to the modern history of Europe through the literature of all its peoples. In the end I was advised to go to Paris. The sceptre of history, I was told, had definitely passed from the Germans to the French. Moreover, at the École des

Chartes I would obtain instruction, not then made available in Oxford, in palaeography and diplomatic. The project unrolled by the talker was so exhilarating, the subjects so spacious and splendid, that I did not hesitate a moment before taking his advice. To Paris, then, I went in September 1889, with introductions to Renan and Taine, and with the resolve to sit at the feet of the French masters of historical science. To the best of my belief no Oxford man had preceded me in that quest. I was the first of a long series, the first to break with the established tradition that post-graduate study in historical science could only profitably be carried on among the Germans.

Paris

THERE is in Paris a *via sacra*, a street of streets. It is
the old Roman Road, which cleaves the Island of
the City and climbs the hill of the Latin Quarter, past
the shabby Rue du Fouarre, where Dante may have
studied, past the Collège de France and the Sorbonne,
leaving the Panthéon on the left and the Odéon Theatre
on the right, and receiving, as it nears the tower of the
old Jacobite house, the name of the Rue St. Jacques.
At 151 bis Rue St. Jacques, a dignified old-fashioned
mansion of the age of Louis Quinze standing at the back
of a slatternly courtyard and thus withdrawn from the
noise and stir of the town, Monsieur and Madame
Casaubon maintained a genteel pension. It was here
that I alighted and spent the first few months of my
initiation into the ways of the University of Paris and
its student quarter. My host was a retired civil servant,
handsome, empty-headed, and, since his working days
were over, entitled to indolence, but stretching indolence
to a point which must seldom be attained by hale and
robust middle life. His lineage was good—he boasted
descent from the great Renaissance scholar—his manners
courtly, his chief pleasure every evening after dinner
to take his cigarette into the street and to sip coffee and
cognac at a neighbouring café with his old cronies. Yet
he experienced at least one literary emotion. He remembered how his father, who had made the Russian cam-

paign under Napoleon, would read out to his children the successive instalments of Thiers' *History of the Consulate and the Empire*, and how coming upon the famous description of the horrors of the Moscow retreat he broke down in an irrepressible flood of tears. As the old fellow touched upon this episode of his boyhood a rare flash of eloquence came into his handsome brown eyes and, shaken out of his habitual placidity, he became for the moment, or felt himself to be, a partner with his dead father in that distant and heroic tragedy.

The mainstay of the establishment was Alexandrine, his wife. If ever there was a heroine it was this valiant, industrious, ever cheerful lady, in a golden wig, who regulated every detail of her large household, kept an infant school, and appeared every night at dinner fresh, amiable, full of sprightly conversation, and as if she had nothing else to do in life but to amuse at table some twenty young men. I have never met anyone who did not admire this capable and most understanding representative of the cultured *bourgeoisie* of France. The inertia of the husband, the brilliant and enjoying activity of the wife, made a piquant contrast.

Among my fellow *pensionnaires* there was one whom the Casaubons held in peculiar and well-deserved regard. Charles Le Sage was a student at the École Libre des Sciences Politiques, and ambitious of entering the inspectorate of finance, when I first made his acquaintance at the friendly dinner table in the Rue St. Jacques. His conversation was brilliant and his knowledge of English politics seemed to me astonishing. That a Frenchman junior to myself should know so much that was of vital importance to my own country of which I, despite all my Oxford education, was profoundly ignorant, filled me with humiliation. Le Sage was as well versed in Hansard as I was in Aristotle. He had chapter and verse for every leading sentiment of our great political gladiators. He knew our Budgets by heart. Our diplomacy, the weakness and strength of our foreign ministers, the political and economic history of contemporary Europe, had been imparted to him on a methodical plan under a scheme of education which had been devised after the Franco-Prussian War to repair the deficiencies in French political knowledge. No better course of instruction for a public servant could be conceived. We had at that time nothing like it in England. Yet the conditions of public life in France were such that Le Sage, brilliant as an official and accomplished as a writer on economics, has never been able to find his way into the Chamber. He stood twice and was twice defeated. After that he was sickened by the atmosphere of French elections. His adversaries bought up the local press and showered calumnies on his mother and sister, and as the law provided no effective redress Le Sage refused to face the electors again.

It was a lovely autumn, warm and still, with golden days and silvery nights, and having allowed myself a month before the university opened to recover my use of the French tongue I explored every nook and cranny

of the Latin Quarter, drinking in the spirit of old Paris
from medieval books and buildings. It was the year of
the Exhibition. Paris was full of foreign visitors, but
of these we saw and heard little in the Latin Quarter.
'You Englishmen', observed Renan on my first meeting
him, 'think of Paris as a great fair, a place of frivolity
and amusement. I tell you it is nothing of the sort. It
is the hardest working place in the world.' The more I
saw of Paris the more true I felt this observation to
be. At Oxford work was moderate, broken by long
spells of healthy exercise and social intercourse. The
French standard, exacted by competition and self-
imposed on all ambitious young men, was of an altogether different order of severity. Such ardour as that
which prevailed among my fellow students in history
was new to me. I had not known what work could be
until I found myself among them.

My plan was to be desultory, to read here, there, and
everywhere, to sample professors in the most widely
divergent topics, to multiply my points of interest as
rapidly as possible, to find out what the great discovering
men were after, what historical ideas were creating
excitement, what periods offered the most attractive
and congenial fields of study. I went to the École des
Chartes for palaeography, to Longnon at the Collège de
France for the geography of Gaul, to Charles Bémont
at the École des Hautes Études for Medieval English
Chronicles, to Albert Sorel at the École Libre des
Sciences Politiques for Modern European History. My

professors were admirable, both for the solidity of their learning and for the technique of their exposition. More particularly am I indebted to my old master Charles Bémont, author of a first-rate life of Simon de Montfort, the editor of the Gascon rolls, and one of the editors for more years than I can recall of the *Revue Historique*. My first historical lecture in French (upon the Chronicles of Rishanger) was delivered at his instigation and at his encouragement. He was a great teacher, disinterested, laborious, and exacting. In France, where English history was not then a popular subject, he was long unrecognized, and only after many years of waiting was this magnificent savant admitted into the Institut de France.

Knowledge and experience poured in from many other quarters. The intellectual giants of the French world were at that time Taine and Renan. To both of these great men I was fortunate enough to have introductions. Each was a man of genius, who stamped himself upon the minds of the younger generation. Taine was a methodizing exponent of applied psychology who combined in a singular degree poetic feeling with logical rigour. Renan was a religious historian of infinite delicacy and vast learning. Each was a rationalist in religion and a conservative in politics. In his erudite work on the *Origins of Contemporary France* Taine explored the ideas of the French Revolution. Renan, travelling over wider ground, recounted the origins of Christianity. The general influence of these two powerful and different minds was, I think, at its height when I settled in Paris in the autumn of 1889. The Taines, who were well to do, lived at 23 Rue Cassette, a spacious house in an old-fashioned street near the Luxembourg Gardens, and here received their friends every Monday evening during the winter months. Here I would meet Leconte de Lisle, Gaston Boissier, James Darmesteter, the brilliant Zend scholar, and his beautiful and gifted English wife (*née* Mary Robinson), Gaston Paris, the master of French medieval literature, and many other scholars and notabilities in the world of letters. The charm and brilliance of my gifted host and hostess and their intelligent daughter helped to bring the most out of every guest. The conversation was gay and intelligent, intellectual without pedantry, ardent without fanaticism. All enjoyed talking and no one shrank from talking about difficult and important things.

At that time Paris was much excited by the remarkable results which Charcot, the great psychiatrist, had obtained at the Salpêtrière, through his experiments on hysterical patients. So striking were they that to some philosophers, and notably to Binet, they seemed to provide the basis of a new psychology. Taine was much impressed by Charcot's work, and hearing that I was contemplating an historical career urged me to embark upon a three-years course of medicine under that great master. He pointed out that history was made by men, that men had bodies, that bodies were now healthy, now disordered, and that the state of the body inevitably

K

affected the action of the mind. The study of the human body, then, was part of the historian's duty—an important part, a much neglected part. The accidents of health had more to do with the march of great events than was ordinarily suspected. A background of psychological knowledge was therefore as necessary to an historian as an acquaintance with geography and economics. After three years at the Salpêtrière I should be in a position to view the past from a scientific angle and to make new and valuable contributions to knowledge.

I could not afford to spare three years to medicine, and doubt whether the time, had it been mine to give, would have been well expended on so elaborate a course. But my experience leads me to think that Taine was clearly justified in his contention that physical causes have been unduly neglected by historians and that they deserve in future to have more attention paid to them. How often during the War of 1914–18 was it not clear that statesmen, generals, and admirals became suddenly less efficient through physical fatigue? The great Lord Cromer was wont to attribute the British conquest of the Sudan to a sore throat which rendered him so speechless during General Gordon's visit to Cairo that he was unable to impress upon that officer's mind the instructions of the Cabinet in London.

Of Renan, then a resident professor at the Collège de France, I retain two impressions. First I see him a fat, squat, broad-shouldered old man, looking like a benevolent toad, who rolls into a crowded little lecture-room, seats himself at the end of a table, where he opens an old Hebrew Bible, and then with a look round his audience of professors, students, and ladies of fashion, pours out a stream of vivid, malicious, melodious French to the accompaniment of intermittent chuckles of delight from his enthralled audience. 'Mesdames et Messieurs', he begins, 'nous abordons aujourd'hui le prophète Daniel.' Or 'Daniel était un vieux sage', and then with a pause and a twinkle, 'un vieux sage apocryphe'. I do not think that many of his audiences were in a state to profit by the old man's learning. It was not zeal for the Hebrew Bible which packed the lecture-room, but the fame of the lecturer. 'Le Père Renan' was a Parisian mode, but a not altogether senseless one, for though he spoke on abstruse themes he spoke in a way which all might appreciate. His *causeries*, poured out from a full mind with an air of artless meditation, were of so subtle and exquisite a texture, and fell upon the ear with such seductive melody, that even the profane were compelled to enjoy and admire.

Later he received me in his study with all the urbanity of one who had been a Roman priest. We talked of Charcot and of his experiments in telepathy, at that time a popular topic of conversation. Renan warned me to be sceptical: 'You must remember', he said, 'that hysterical patients have a strong tendency to deceive.' Then we drifted away to discourse of foreign travel. Renan admired the medieval pilgrimages and wished the custom could be revived. Throwing himself back in his chair and closing his eyes, he allowed himself to float away into a kind of soothing dreamland, seeing in a succession of little pictures the pilgrimages which he would like to make and communicating to his visitor something of his own enjoyment of them. As an entertainment for a shy young foreigner, nothing could have been better. At the end of it the great man came to the door and helped me on with my coat.

Many years afterwards I had a long talk about Renan with Sabatier, the famous authority on St. Francis. Sabatier was born in Nîmes, a great Protestant stronghold. So fanatical was his mother in her Protestantism that she would draw down the blinds rather than that any inmate of her household should set eyes upon a Catholic procession passing along the street. As a very small boy Sabatier was distressed by the thought of these wicked Catholics, creatures so wicked that it was pollution to gaze upon them. Very secretly he determined to make those wicked Catholics better, to convert them, but first to know all about them. So he would steal into Catholic churches, listen to Catholic music, study Catholic ritual. Very soon he became so learned in matters of ritual that priests came to consult him. Then he sought a deeper kind of learning. He became a university student in Paris, and one day, since his subject was theology, found himself standing right at the back of Renan's lecture-room, as I had done. Something in his appearance, perhaps his rare personal beauty and flaming dark eyes, attracted the old man's attention.

'Avez-vous compris?' he asked. 'Pas un mot, Monsieur', was the reply. Thereupon, to his intense astonishment and delight, this raw young provincial student was taken up into the great man's study and treated to such a lecture on theology as he would never have thought possible. At the end he started to take his leave. It was raining hard. He had no great-coat, no umbrella, and his poor garret was the other side of Paris. Renan escorted him home, holding his umbrella over him all the way and all the time talking like a God. At the end of their journey Sabatier was too shy to interrupt the talk and so back they walked to the Collège de France and back again across Paris to the student's lodgings, the famous old man steadily holding up the umbrella and steadily talking, the enraptured young student trotting by his side. As may be imagined, from that time onwards Sabatier was Renan's slave. It was to Renan that he owed the chief inspiration of his life. 'You wish', said the great savant, 'to reconcile the Catholic and Protestant Churches. Study St. Francis. He is what Catholics and Protestants have in common.'

The École des Chartes, then presided over by Paul Meyer, the great Romance scholar, is primarily a vocational school for the training of French archivists. The spirit of the great Benedictine scholars pervaded this austere seminary of all the scholarly virtues. 'Remember, gentlemen', remarked Léon Gautier, that ardent and delightful editor of the *Chanson de Roland*, when he wished to spur on our flagging energies, 'that the great

Ducange worked for fourteen hours on his wedding-day.'
The ceremony at the *Soutenance des Thèses*, when the
young men were called upon to defend the final exercise
upon which their title to be called Archiviste Paléo-
graphe depended, was enough to strike awe into the
beholder. The three venerable judges, with the Olympian
figure of Léopold Delisle, the Librarian of the Bibliothèque Nationale, presiding, sat on the dais, discharging
a formidable battery of questions at their victim below,
while professors and students and friends crowded round
to hear the battle of wits. Little quarter was given or
expected on these occasions. Woe to the student who
failed to interpret an abbreviation, to give a date, to
identify a quotation, or to master all the relevant
sources. The tribunal had been over his work with
a microscope. The smallest sign of slipshod scholarship
caught its eye and provoked a censure.

Since, however, it was no part of my plan to qualify
as an archivist, this intensive discipline in French
medieval history was only allowed to absorb a small part
of my time. The École des Chartes supplied one side
only of my historical training. Nor was it the most
important side. The past cannot be reconstructed by
men whose knowledge of life is solely derived from
documents. Old papers do not tell the whole story;
they may not tell the most important part of the story.
The historian who contents himself with presenting to
his readers a *cento* of texts and packs his pages with
information not because it is significant but because it

is available, does not truly fulfil his office. His books will doubtless be learned; but they will lack the perspective and the insight into reality which makes the past instructive to living men. Historical scholarship has its own special function to perform, but a fine historical scholar may nevertheless be a poor historian. Not without warrant did my wise friend Taine advise me against excessive devotion to the École des Chartes.

One day that autumn the newspapers announced the death of one of those rare beings who was at once, and in the most complete sense, a scholar and an historian. Fustel de Coulanges was a name already well known to me, for most Oxford men reading for Greats had been recommended to profit from the brilliant lucidity, the bold outlines and vast learning of *La Cité Antique*, but of Fustel's all-important medieval work there was at that time little knowledge in England outside a narrow circle of specialists who, like Maitland, were working in the field of early social and legal history. Imagine then my delight on receiving from Mandell Creighton an invitation (prompted by Maitland) that I should celebrate Fustel in the pages of the *English Historical Review*. Fustel had travelled on the high road which leads from the ancient to the modern world. It was exactly the route which I proposed to follow. Hastily devouring the noble volumes in which that wonderful scholar traces the continuity of Latin influence in Gaul, I made my first experiment in authorship (January 1890).

The Hôtel de France et de Lorraine, once much frequented by quiet country gentry of the Royalist persuasion, and standing almost at the angle of the Rue de Beaune and the Quai Voltaire, has now, like many another pleasant old-fashioned building, been improved off the face of the map. Yet in 1889 this modest inn enjoyed a certain renown among visitors of a studious taste and temperament. George Eliot used to stay here. So too did James Russell Lowell, that witty American *littérateur*, on whose recommendation I was drawn to exchange my distant quarters in the Mont Ste-Geneviève for this central yet secluded hostelry. Here I found myself in a nest of artists. Among my fellow lodgers were A. H. Studd (known as Peter) and William Rothenstein and Kenneth Frazier, a gifted young American artist. Peter, an Eton and Cambridge friend of my cousin George Duckworth, was already known to me. He was the most diffident and delightful of men. The conventions of Eton and Cambridge, where, like his brothers, he was distinguished as a cricketer, had not dimmed the poetry of his simple and ardent nature. That he was gifted beyond the ordinary was made evident when he tried his hand at an original composition in oils. In the management of tongue and pen he had little skill. His thoughts could not express themselves in words, and examinations must have presented an almost insuperable horror. But by degrees he discovered a vocation in which the most inarticulate might excel. Far later than most men he made painting a profession.

When I ran across him in Paris he was in the first flush of enthusiasm for his new-found art. His enjoyment of it was infectious, and had his executive power been equal to his sense of poetic inspiration he would have taken a high rank among the painters of his time.

Will Rothenstein, when I first met him in Studd's company, was a tiny lad of seventeen, already wearing large horn spectacles, and a marvel of precocious virtuosity. He moved with incredible ease and nimbleness in every medium. He perorated, he wrote, he drew, he painted. By the cosmopolitan crowd who toiled away in the noisy, crowded studios of the Académie Julian he was regarded as the infant prodigy, the coming man. Again and again he won competitions against artists many years his senior. His enthusiastic vitality, quick wit, and droll imagination made him a universal favourite. 'C'est un artiste au bout des ongles', said Rodin. Perhaps if he had had less all-round facility he would have accomplished more as a painter. Yet his achievement has been considerable, alike as artist and author. Few of the notabilities of his age have contrived to escape his assiduous and skilful pencil. Even town-councillors have been swayed by his eloquence. In later life he made a reputation as a capable and inspiring Director of the Royal College of Art and as the author of delightful volumes of autobiography, wherein may be found a faithful and engaging picture of that artistic circle in Paris, into which he was plunged as a raw provincial from Bradford, and from which he emerged

L

having tasted many forms of enjoyment and learned much about the ways, both good and evil, of mankind.

A very different character and a most valuable element in our group was Ludwig von Hofmann. This handsome, grave, aristocratic Bavarian was older and riper than most of the art students who gathered in the evening to perorate *de omni scibili* in Studd's salon. Of the fine technical qualities which were afterwards destined to win for von Hofmann renown in his native country, I could form no estimate. His enthusiasm, however, for the most recent developments of French art was genuine and unmistakable, his nature wholesome and magnanimous. I could see that the military humiliation of France, the hospitable metropolis of the painter's art, caused in him a certain malaise. Like Byron he was impressed by the deep melancholy of history.

It is an education to be inducted by artist friends into their earthly paradise of light and shadow and soft gradations of shifting and delicate tints. For my companions a plain wall of plaster in a dirty malodorous street might be a source of positive delight. Let a mauve or pearl-grey shadow be thrown on the drab white superficies, and the object for them was transfigured. In my walks abroad in Paris my attention was continually directed to the miracles wrought by sun and shade. My painting friends lived for colour and found nothing so dull or so ugly but that a change of light might invest it with loveliness. They would proclaim the beauty of factory chimneys, gasometers, and dustbins. If I was not equal to their raptures they brought new ranges of pleasure within my reach.

Impressionism was in the first flush of its fame. The God whom we were taught to worship was Monet, of whom Clemenceau, a great friend, tells the story that the artist standing by the bedside of his dying mistress could see nothing but the beautiful violet shadow on her temple. There was a picture of a pine tree by this gifted painter in Goupil's window, in which the separate tints were so brilliantly distinguished that they could be seen on the other side of the Boulevard. To this we made a pious pilgrimage, as also to the frescoes of Besnard in the École de Pharmacie and to those of Puvis de Chavannes in the Panthéon. The fashionable painters of the day were loaded with our denunciation. To have a picture hanging in the Salon was regarded as a patent humiliation. I was not myself equipped to join in the nocturnal denunciations of my friends, but I agreed with them in thinking the Salon disappointing. 'My compatriots', Rodin observed to me once in explanation, 'have lost the art of admiration.' But if that faculty was lost by Frenchmen it was very marked in my artist friends from England, America, and Germany. Indifferent as the Salon may have been, the artistic influence of Paris was to an amazing extent predominant through Europe. Save in England and Spain the art schools of Paris dictated the fashion.

Two stormy petrels were scudding over the political

waters, one was Boulanger, the other Déroulède. I was out among the excited crowd during the critical night when the French electorate voted down the showy but ineffectual General who proposed to revise the Constitution, and was thought to be the harbinger of war. The wide and menacing popularity of this incompetent politician—a popularity which he fomented by pandering to the lowest anti-Semite prejudices of the mob—was an indication of the continuing malaise of France under a régime which was thought to be over timid and tolerant of defeat.

The loss of Alsace-Lorraine rankled in all minds. Every politician and every measure were judged in the light of the German question. The winning of a new Colonial Empire in the Far East was used as a stick to beat Jules Ferry. 'Le Tonquinois' was a term of bitter abuse. There were many who thought it folly to squander blood and treasure in distant waters, when the all-important prize of French policy was near at hand. The fiery Déroulède, who had fought in 1870, was an active propagandist for the policy which ultimately led through the Franco-Russian Alliance to the Great War. When he came to ask Renan to subscribe to the *Ligue des Patriotes*, founded to keep alive the idea of the war of revenge, the old sage replied, 'Young man, France is dying, do not trouble her agony.' Such pessimism was common. The faith in the national intellect was as high as the confidence in the political destiny of France was low. 'Tous les députés sont vendus,' was the common opinion of the students. The Chamber had not recovered from the shock of the Panama scandal.

It was not, indeed, until I immersed myself in the atmosphere of Paris that I began to realize the perils which were still in store for civilization. In England we had been brought up in the idea of a stable peace, an expanding commerce, a progressive and steady advance in well-being and right reason throughout the world. Our political struggles were keen but about matters of secondary importance. Most of us believed with Herbert Spencer that the world was passing from a military into an industrial state of existence. In France there was none of that island security. Revolution and war were present possibilities. At a political meeting in one of the faubourgs, which I attended from curiosity, the speaker was forced by the clamour of his audience to apologize to the Republicans for his use of the word 'Monsieur' and to the atheists for his exclamation 'Mon Dieu'. Beneath the polished surface of French life the tradition of the Jacobin was still alive and ready to burst into flame. My hosts had begun to take notice of England. Everyone was talking of a book with an arresting title, *A quoi tient la supériorité des Anglo-Saxons?* Taine's remarkable study of English literature and Boutmy's brilliant sketch of English constitutional development answered a general demand for more knowledge about the neighbouring island across the Channel. Albion remained perfidious. We were not popular; but we had become respected. Of the foreign pictures displayed that year at the Exhibition the English alone occasioned the surprise and admiration of the crowd.

Meanwhile, the intellectual currents ran strongly against romance. The young men had deserted Alexandre Dumas and Georges Sand for the masters of realism. Balzac was a demi-god. The praise of Flaubert's *Madame Bovary* was on all lips. Here was that serious documentation of life which should be the end of all literature, and in Flaubert the sublime instrument of the French language wielded with a scholar's scruple. My contemporaries were proud of the novelist whose happiness was said to have been poisoned by the two dependent genitives, *une couronne des fleurs d'orange*, which had found their way into a sentence of his masterpiece. The older men who liked flowing, easy, romantic French were unconverted. 'Madame Sand', said Renan, 'will be read three hundred years hence', but the prevailing tone was that of the melancholy Edmond de Goncourt, himself trained in the École des Chartes, whose journal, based upon the experience of a lifetime, presents a faithful picture of the literary and artistic society of Paris (on its less learned and serious side) which I was privileged in my early manhood for a brief period to enjoy.

Germany

DURING the last two decades of the nineteenth century the German universities enjoyed a wide reputation for freedom, courage, and learning. To sit at the feet of some great German Professor, absorbing his publications, listening to his lectures, working in his seminary, was regarded as a valuable, perhaps as a necessary passport to the highest kind of academic career. Every year young graduates from our universities would repair to Berlin and Heidelberg, to Göttingen and Bonn, to Jena and Tübingen. The names of the German giants, of Ranke and Mommsen, of Wilamowitz and Lotze, were sounded again and again by their admiring disciples in British lecture-rooms. We learned that the great figures of the Augustan period of German literature had been followed by two generations of perhaps even more remarkable men, who had given new life to every branch of human knowledge. We were adjured to learn the tongue (in my case a basis had been laid at school), to read the classics, and to venerate the achievements of this superlative and indispensable race. And as we were prepared to like and admire the Germans, so we were disposed naively to assume that the Germans were equally willing to like and admire us.

It was in accordance with these predispositions, but rather with the idea of perfecting my knowledge of the German language and of seeing something of German student life than of worshipping at any peculiar shrine, that I elected to supplement my year in France with a spell at the University of Göttingen. The commendation of friends, the respect owing to the Hanoverian accent, the reputation among British historians of the University of Waitz and Pauli, the delicious satire of Heine, combined to determine my preference for the Georgia Augusta University in Göttingen. I travelled out with an introduction to an ancient Hanoverian noblewoman, and under the roof of Frau von Dachenhausen learned something of the quality of that old Hanoverian civilization which had met its doom in the field of Langensalza in 1866. My hostess was an elegant, rosy little widow, as gay as a butterfly, whose daughters were out in the world and whose life consisted in the discharge of numberless little duties in her pleasant house and garden, enlivened by the solemn routine of an afternoon whist drive. So domestic was she that she had never, though naturally of a benevolent disposition, entered a poor home or contributed to a charity, for these were the duties, she explained, of the municipality; so domestic that although a pious Lutheran she nevertheless attended Church only twice a year; so domestic that I do not remember to have seen her open a book or a newspaper. The university she regarded with indifference and some slight tincture of conservative disdain. As for foreign politics, they were summed up in a strong detestation of the Prussians against whom her family had been arrayed in battle. Yet this little lady, whose mind was so empty and whose interests were so contracted never, I am persuaded, had a dull moment in the day. She lived in a continual paroxysm of happiness. Eager prattle poured from her lips as she tripped nimbly about her business. She would watch a fly on the window-pane with the delight of a child. She ate her unappetizing food with rapturous enjoyment. Every duty was a pleasure. She was never cross or worried. A happier or more contented and self-sufficient old lady it would be difficult to meet. The *Sturm und Drang* of the heroic age had passed her by. She might have been a character out of a German *Cranford*.

My reception among the students was marked by all the cordial friendliness and open-hearted simplicity which I had been led to expect from the German race. They admitted me to their clubs, invited me to their Kneipe or drinking feasts, and allowed me to participate in the club walks into the country which degenerated into protracted and tedious sessions in some neighbouring beer house. The social prestige which in Oxford belonged to the great cricketer or oarsman was in Göttingen the reward for slashed cheeks or deep potations. Nor could a professor more surely win his way to the hearts of his disciples than by appearing in their Kneipe and swallowing pot after pot of beer into the small hours of the morning. Of industry there was no lack. The veritably studious eclipsed our English standards in their obdurate application. But it was far otherwise with the roistering *Corps Studenten*. Such idleness as theirs would never

M

have been tolerated even in one of our royal foundations at Oxford or Cambridge.

One day in the late autumn of 1890 a fellow member of the *Historische Verein* explained to me with the utmost friendliness that Germany regarded Britain as her eternal enemy and predestined victim. We Britons had won an Empire by good fortune, when Germany was asleep, and we should lose it inevitably (the more so because ever since 1832 the British nation had become degenerate) now that Germany was fully awake. Britain was Carthage. Germany was Rome. Even if the first Punic war was not successful there would be other Punic wars to follow. Germany aspired to rule the world. Britain stood in her way. The stage was set for a great, an inexorable struggle. My young friend related these beliefs with polite composure, adding that it was known in Germany (though I should be in my rights in denying it) that Queen Victoria was a dipsomaniac (why, if not in search of the national beverage, should she go to Scotland?) and her eldest son (apparently confused with a distinguished nobleman) a kleptomaniac. That this discomposing disclosure was not, as I was at first inclined to think, a young man's sally, soon became clear. The doctrine of the Punic wars was abroad through Germany. Its fountain-head, so far as I could discover, was the deaf, violent, Saxon Professor, Heinrich von Treitschke, who was then drawing large audiences to Berlin by his eloquent diatribes against Great Britain. The native kindliness of the German student remained unaffected

by these formidable prospects. Perhaps he was the more
ready to be indulgent to the Englishman since the ruin
of his unfortunate country was so clearly inscribed in
the book of fate.

To the good-natured barbarism of my student associates there was one comforting exception. Fritz Keutgen,
a *Privatdozent* in medieval history, was mild, serious,
and cultured, combining with professional ambitions of
the most severe type a taste for poetry, music, and
pictures. With this fair-haired and romantic companion
I roamed the Hanoverian woodlands, exchanging dreams
and notions and learning more of the inner Germany
than formal lectures could give me. In later years my
disinterested friend made a name for himself as a writer
on German medieval history. The arid theme provoked
fiery controversies, and Keutgen, though a poor man,
declined a lucrative Chair in an American university
rather than leave a reputation behind him to be torn
to tatters by envious compatriots. In the fierce mael-
strom of competition, which was then a disagreeable
feature of German academic life, little quarter was given
or received.

A spring holiday spent between Weimar and Dresden
rounded off my first experience of Germany. Having
read much of Goethe during the winter, I had imagined
that there was little more which a visit to the *Goethe-Haus*
could teach me. An absurd delusion. The size of Goethe,
the vast span of his artistic and intellectual interests,
the fullness and energy of his titanic nature are never

so clear to the mind as in the home in which he lived and worked (with so little of material comfort) and stored that huge miscellaneous collection of fossils and plants, of engravings and statues, of the literatures alike of the West and the Orient which attest the workings of his universal mind. The man emerges from his home, whole and entire, as Gladstone from the libraries and noble trees of Hawarden.

Wagner, his reputation not yet assailed by Nietzsche's brilliant pen, ruled the musical world. Every night during my stay at Dresden I attended the Opera and listened to Malten and Scheidemantel, then at the height of their vocal powers, in Wagnerian Opera. I am no musician. The spell which Wagnerian music then cast over me has long since passed away. But during that spring I felt that Wagner had divined the inner spirit of primitive German history and had given me a comprehension of the forces which from the first have governed the vast and tumultuous movement of this people, so savage and sentimental, so virile and laborious, so passionate and profound, so perseveringly dedicated to the ideals of primitive heroism which had been pre-served in the poetry recording the early wanderings and struggles of the race.

As in France so in Germany my reading in history and literature had been wide and desultory. I had learned something of Europe, but of the requirements of the Modern History School at Oxford, in which I was now invited to take a hand, nothing whatever. This lacuna in my education was filled during a short reading party at Southwold by A. L. Smith, then the leading history tutor at Balliol. Smith was a born teacher of everything under the sun. He taught me to skate, he taught me to ride a bicycle; from him I learned what pellicules of history an undergraduate might be expected to absorb, and how best the fastidious appetite of the most evasive might be tempted. Smith was too deeply immersed in pushing young gentlemen over examination fences to be a profound scholar; but if he lacked the learning he had the vision, the humour, and the animation of a true historian. The men and women of the past came alive in his mind. Such skill as I acquired in the technique of college teaching was learnt from him.

With such preparation I addressed myself to the task of teaching Modern History at Oxford. 'It will take you ten years', observed Frank Bright, the Master of University, 'to feel comfortable in the saddle.' Again and again, in my struggles to keep abreast of the march of knowledge I was reminded of that wise but over-sanguine prediction.

The Academic Life

To an ambitious young Englishman, who succeeds in winning a College Fellowship, a life of lettered ease appears at first to offer a prospect of endless enchantments. His appetite for knowledge is fresh and keen. He is powerfully excited by the beauties of literature. The joy of experimenting with his pen on paper, of 'revelling', as Disraeli calls it, 'in the sunshine of composition', is very strong. He dreams of writing plays and novels or great masterpieces of history, or elegant essays, and is bewildered by the multiplicity of writers who simultaneously exert upon his mind a powerful attraction. To master and to expound to others some important aspect of human knowledge is an ambition which fulfils for many years the cravings of his nature. A difficult book, presenting a real gymnastic problem to the intellect, can keep him bound to his desk for hours so that he either misses his midday meal or works far into the morning. In the years between twenty and thirty the pleasures of the intellect may well be all-sufficient. Every hour opens fresh prospects and brings fresh conquests. In some moods the life of learning appears to satisfy every need and every ambition.

Yet if I may judge from my own experience there is always a haunting feeling that learning and scholarship and the lettered life can bring content only if combined with some more practical form of active service to the community. Men of the highest genius do not, I daresay, feel this, but the ordinary Englishman craves for action, and even the most strenuous form of action involved in educational work ceases after some years to fulfil his need. When the first excitements of the intellectual life have worn themselves out, and the pleasure of the chase is abated, he struggles to find an escape from the library into the open air of the common life. Administration, politics, travel, philanthropy lure him away from his books.

My own ambitions as a young Oxford graduate were firstly to make myself an effective teacher of history, and secondly, to maintain the repute of British scholarship by making sooner or later some contribution to historical knowledge. Clio is an exacting muse. To combine effective historical teaching with real research imposes a severe drain on the energies. And yet there was always the tantalizing, haunting feeling that youth was passing away with its pleasures, its opportunities, its call for practical service, and that the real salt of life, only to be tasted in the animating surges of the outer world, had been missed. These thoughts were sharply brought home to me one evening in August 1892, during a visit to the Gilbert Murrays, who had taken a house for the summer in the little hamlet of Kincraig. It so happened that John Morley and his wife were also established a few doors away, and that on many an evening the two households interchanged visits and discussed literature and history to their hearts' content. It was my first occasion to meet Morley, whom I had long admired on many grounds political and literary, and since he was then engaged on a study of Guicciardini, an author with whom I also had some acquaintance, we instantly found common ground. It was a delightful holiday. The weather was lovely, the scenery was beautiful, the talk eager and wide-ranging. On the last evening of our visit, as Murray and I were taking our leave, Morley said, 'I will send you away with a text', and kneeling on the floor, read out from a well-worn little copy of Bain's life of J. S. Mill by the light of a single candle the master's prescription for a happy life; that we should never expect from life more than life can give, and that the happy life should be three parts practical. Morley himself had been drawn into politics by the spectacle of poverty seen from his windows in Lincoln's Inn. He thought that the time had come when his two young friends should come out into the open. The hint was not lost. The ship of State, though we did not then know it, was rapidly sailing into dangerous waters, and the time was shortly to come when Murray and I were to be swept into the centre of public affairs by circumstances which neither of us could then foresee.

The Board of Education

ONE day in the late autumn of 1916 I received an invitation from Major (now Lord) Davies to breakfast in his rooms to meet Lloyd George, then Secretary of State for War in the Asquith administration. I had met Ll. G. some years before, when he was staying with Sir John Rhys, the Principal of Jesus, and he remembered to my surprise all about that meeting. Though we breakfasted early the Minister had already had an interview with the mother of a wounded officer and arrived hot with her complaints of military red tape. It appeared, for the talk at table centred entirely round foreign affairs, that Ll. G. wished to ascertain my views as to the settlement of Europe after the war. His own opinion was that the nature of the peace would depend upon the course of the campaign. 'If the Kaiser and Hindenburg', he observed, 'were present at this table I would give them a tip. I would say to them, "win victories if you like in the East, but get yourself beaten as soon as possible on the Western Front. Otherwise you will have a very hard peace".' That no doubt was true. The character of the Peace Settlement would certainly be affected by the nature and duration of the war. As things stood, however, I suggested that the Allies should be contented with the liberation of the occupied French and Belgian territory, with the return of Alsace-Lorraine to France, the cession of the Trentino and Trieste to

Italy, and with a federal constitution for the Austrian Empire. I could see, however, that Ll. G., with his persistent belief in small nations, had already made up his mind to the break-up of the Hapsburg Empire, and that he regarded this as a necessary and salutary step towards the democratic organization of Europe. On the grievances of the Czechs, the Slovaks, the Roumans, he spoke with eloquence. I was not, however, convinced that these grievances might not then be met by a wise scheme of federation. Two years later my solution was impossible. The old Empire had crashed to the ground, the insurgent nations were in power. The statesmen at Versailles had no option but to recognize the accomplished fact. Had peace been made in 1916, a federal Austrian Empire might have survived to police the Danubian region, but after the shattering Italian victory of Vittorio Veneto, in which it may be remembered that Lord Cavan with his British divisions led the Italian centre, an Austrian Empire of any kind was out of the question.

At that time nothing was farther from my expectations than that I should ever be summoned to take a share in governing the country. Destiny had called me to preside over the University of Sheffield, and in Sheffield I expected to work out my allotted span. Things turned out otherwise. One cold night in December as I was lying on a sofa shivering with 'flu, a call came through from London. Lloyd George was on the telephone. Could I breakfast with him next day at 9 a.m.? Impossible!

What was the earliest moment at which I could call at the War Office? Midday. At midday I should be expected. It was most important.

Very miserable with a feverish influenza cold, I travelled up to London on a chill wet December morning, surmising but hardly venturing to believe that I might be asked into the Government and doubtful in that event what my answer should be. I had not been following very closely the course of politics in London, but held Asquith in great regard and admiration and was sorry to hear of the fall of his Ministry, and on that account shrank from action which might be interpreted as implying a measure of dissatisfaction with his conduct of the War which I was far from feeling. It was as I supposed. At the War Office I found Lloyd George looking haggard and anxious, together with Bonar Law, whom I then met for the first time. 'I have sent to ask you', began Ll. G. in his most flattering manner, 'to help in the government of this country,' and proceeded to offer me the Board of Education. I urged that I had no parliamentary experience and that in any case Michael Sadler knew more about education than I did. The Prime Minister replied that, although he was not a highly cultivated man like Mr. Asquith, he believed that, being the son of an elementary schoolmaster, he cared more for popular education, and added that we had now reached a point in our history when the country would take more educational reform from an educationalist than from a politician. I confess that this observation seemed

to me to have real force. I told him, however, that I
felt that I could do my work at Sheffield reasonably
well, that my success in Parliament would be doubtful
and that in any case I should not want to mark time in
a government office. 'Would there', I asked, 'be money
for educational reforms and improvements?' I saw that
this was essential. Ll. G. assured me that money would
be forthcoming and that he would give me his personal
support. And so after a conversation with W. N. Bruce
of the Board of Education, and a second interview with
Ll. G. at the War Office in the afternoon and a con-
fabulation with my wife on my return to Sheffield, I
telephoned my acceptance. Though I had many misgivings at the time I have no doubt that my decision
was right. The Prime Minister was as good as his word.
To a Cabinet so largely conservative my educational
proposals must have seemed most extravagant, but the
Prime Minister's strong and constant support, for which
I can never be too grateful, ensured the acceptance of
every plan which I placed before my colleagues. In
Balfour, too, the cause of education had an enlightened
and powerful friend.

My first year of office was one of the most anxious and
terrible in history. The Russian Revolution, the Italian
defeat at Caporetto, the mutinies in the French Army,
the huge wastage of good English life in the ill-judged
battle of Paschendaele, above all the U-boat campaign,
which in the early months of 1917 seemed likely to reduce
our island to starvation, constituted a formidable mass

of misfortune. The one countervailing grace was the entry of the United States into the War. Never shall I forget the evening when the news came through. I was dining with the Astors at 4 St. James's Square. The table was spread with the Stars and Stripes, and Mr. Page, the American Ambassador and a noble friend to our country, was there to celebrate with us the event for which he had worked with such persistent and faithful zeal. Wilson's great speech was on all lips. Balfour, who was wont to choose his words carefully, said to me as we walked away that he thought it the greatest speech he had ever read. The next morning, walking to my office, I saw the Stars and Stripes floating by the Union Jack from the Victoria Tower in Westminster in the bright April sky. Yet the most anxious days were still ahead. My brother William had come to the Admiralty to direct the anti-submarine department and, since I was a member of the Cabinet and bound to secrecy, he could reveal to me in the course of our strolls in St. James's Park something of his anxiety. Not that he ever wavered in his splendid confidence that the enemy would ultimately be subdued. His task was, indeed, a terrible one. No member of the British Navy, as Beatty once told me, had a more disturbing or anxious responsibility. He was the first recipient of the heart-rending news of the sinkings at sea, and yet despite the impact of these continuous calamities compelled to exert every intellectual and spiritual resource at his command in devising means for combating the enemy. His cheerful animation, buoyancy, and high courage were beyond praise. On Armistice Day Eric Geddes, then First Lord of the Admiralty, said to me, 'Your brother had more to do with this than anyone'. It was not, I think, an idle compliment, but his juniority in the service (for he was at that time only a Captain) excluded him from recommendation for any reward which would have been commensurate with his service.

The vast expenditure and harrowing anxieties of the time, so far from extinguishing the needs of social progress, helped to promote a widespread feeling for improvement in the general lot of the people. Where war demands of all equal sacrifices, it was felt that to all should be accorded, so far as might be, equal opportunities. The country was in a spending mood and eager to compensate the wastage of war by some real contribution to the arts of peace. As happens in any revolutionary age the educational world was in a state of ferment. For the first time in our national history education was a popular subject and discussed in an atmosphere cleared of religious acrimony. Large audiences were attracted to educational meetings and listened with interest to addresses on the school age and physical training and how best to fit the younger generation for the strain and burden of modern life. In the movement of discussions which proceeded all over the country Sir Robert Blair, the very able Scot who had the post of Education Officer to the London County Council, took a prominent part. Even more influential, though at that time exercising his influence sometimes through speeches in the House of Lords but more continuously in private consultations with the officers of the Board of Education, was Lord Haldane, the great War Minister, who shared to the full the Scottish enthusiasm for education, and having been educated partly in Germany was fully aware of our serious national deficiencies in that regard. His great speech (12 July 1916) in the Lords dwelt upon our shortage of experts and compared us unfavourably with Switzerland and America.

I belonged to a Coalition Government, formed for the purpose of continuing the war. In considering, therefore, what measures I could safely propose to Parliament it was above all things necessary to avoid giving umbrage to either of the great political parties. The last important educational measure which had been placed on the Statute Book was the Act of 1902, which had been framed by Robert Morant, a great civil servant, and passed through the House of Commons by A. J. Balfour after long, tedious, and fiery discussions in which Lloyd George, championing the interests of the Free Churches, had made his reputation as a first-class parliamentary gladiator. Any attempts to revive the fierce controversies of that memorable educational debate would have seriously impaired the cohesion of the Government and wrecked such chances as I might have of making a useful contribution to educational progress. Even then if I had desired to alter the framework of the system which had been designed by Morant, or to modify that part of

it which had aroused most opposition, I should have felt
myself precluded from doing so by the obvious necessity
of preserving the party peace. As a matter of fact I had
no desire to alter the system. I was well content with
a scheme under which the public system of education
in the country was conducted by a partnership between
the Board of Education and the local education authorities. It would have been a senseless extravagance to
buy out the Church schools, and suicidal to derange the
hard-won compromise on the religious question, the
attainment of which in the teeth of intelligent Liberal
opposition had been one of Balfour's finest parliamentary
achievements. The general framework of the Balfour
Act seemed to me to be sound. If the system was not
ideal, if it was very far from being the kind of system
which it would have occurred to any statesman to con-
struct on a *tabula rasa*, it possessed two great advantages. First, it was in actual working. Second, it was
clearly compatible with great improvements and
developments.

One major change might perhaps have been introduced without, in the state of the public mind at that
time, exciting violent controversy. Had I proposed that
the teachers should be made civil servants, that they
should be appointed, paid, and pensioned by the State, I
could probably have carried my point. The suggestion
had been thrown out at more than one educational conference. It offers certain palpable attractions, and for a
moment I toyed with the idea. But on a closer view the

policy disclosed such a prospect of danger to educational freedom and to a wholesome variety of experimentation, such a menace to local responsibility and so formidable an accretion of work and power to the Board at Whitehall, that I dismissed it from my mind. It is better that the teaching body in a country should be ill distributed, unevenly paid, and imperfectly qualified than that it should be thought to march to the orders of a government in London.

Popular opinion pronounced me to be an 'educationalist'. That was a delusion. I had never, save for a week when I was an undergraduate, taught in a school nor addressed myself to a serious study of pedagogic literature. Though for a short time I had served as a member of two education committees, and had acted as Vice-Chancellor in a provincial university, compared with many experienced members of Parliament who had for many years served on such bodies I was a tiro in the problems of educational administration. My true field of study was and had long been the history and literature of Europe, and I should have been more in place as Under-Secretary of State for Foreign Affairs, a position for which I was afterwards considered, than as President of the Board of Education. Nevertheless no one could have had so long an experience of academic life as I without acquiring some familiarity with the best educational thought of the time and some general knowledge of the way in which education was being carried on in the country. My sympathies were democratic. I believed

o

in the open career for talent, and was ambitious of the honour of widening the highway from the elementary school to the university. The thought of young ambition starving for knowledge and stinted in opportunities was very present to my mind, for I had known many such examples in the course of my work as an Oxford tutor, as an occasional resident in Bethnal Green, and as a Sheffield Vice-Chancellor. It seemed to me that a country which closed down formal education for the great bulk of its child population at the age of twelve was allowing human capital to run to waste on a prodigal scale. I felt that education, the most fundamental of all the social services, was susceptible of almost indefinite improvement and that by a real and fortunate chance I had been called upon to improve it.

Henry Sidgwick, the wise Cambridge philosopher, used to say that Governments were always right, meaning, I suppose, that with the resources of the British Civil Service behind him, a minister has little excuse for going wrong. Certainly no minister could have desired more brilliant support than I received during my term of office of nearly six years from the officers of the Board of Education. The enthusiastic spirit of Robert Morant still pervaded the dreary corridors of our repellent dungeon. The men with whom I was privileged to work had faith in their task and never stinted their labour. In some there was a kind of apostolic fervour, in all so far as I could see a high measure of scrupulous competence.

The office was ruled by Amherst Selby Bigge, formerly of the Charity Commission, whose minutes, in their careful balance and elegance of expression and strong practical wisdom; were models of the way in which this kind of work should be done. Bigge had been with me at Winchester. I then admired him as a formidable hero of the football field. He was, after a distinguished undergraduate career, for a time a Student of Christ Church and a philosophy don at University, and the author of several philosophic treatises. There have been few better minds in our Civil Service, or more loyal and efficient servants of public education in our country.

The head of the secondary school department was W. N. Bruce, a man of great charm, distinction, and sagacity whose heart was in his work and who has left his mark not only upon the grant-aided schools which came under his supervision but in a special way upon university education in Wales. The Prime Minister thought all the world of Bruce and scolded me for not having recommended him for an honour on his retirement. My reply was that I understood that a Grand Cross in an order of Knighthood would be unacceptable. Some years later he was offered and accepted the Companionship of Honour.

The Civil Service in our country, drawing as it does upon the best talent of the university, has always been rich in scholarship and literary powers. From time to time it has even sheltered a poet. Matthew Arnold, whose admirable reports emphasized for the first time the grave deficiencies in our provision for secondary schools, was an inspector of schools. For a short time, Herbert Trench, a lesser poet than Matthew Arnold, but the author of those exquisite verses, 'She cometh not when Noon is on the Roses', fingered some office files at the Board of Education under the stern and disapproving eye of Morant. The growing mass of administrative work to be done did not extinguish the cult of the Muses. In my time literary scholarship was brilliantly represented by J. W. Mackail and E. K. Chambers, each of whom, while discharging to the full his duties as a public servant, found time to achieve fame in the world of learning and letters. In my private secretaries, always so important to a hard-worked minister, I was most fortunate. Two of them, the best of friends, to my grief died in the prime of life; Frank Oates, Harrovian cricketer, Nottinghamshire squire, and famous as a partridge shot, though making no pretensions to intellectual brilliance, was a man of saintly character and sagacious judgement who was beloved by all who knew him; and Alan Kidd, who was only prevented by wrecked health from reaching the highest distinction in the Civil Service, and also, as I believe, in the field of literary criticism, had he chosen so to employ his gifted and fastidious pen. Of talent other than literary there was abundance. W. R. Barker and H. W. Orange were towers of strength, the one in the legal and the other in the finance department. George Newman, the dominating and driving force in the School Medical Service and later the first chief officer in the Ministry of Health, was an ideal exponent of the practice and principles of preventive medicine. Two of the Chief Inspectors were men of high qualifications, the one an Ireland Scholar from Oxford, the other a Senior Wrangler from Cambridge, a third, O. M. Edwards, a man of genius who, after winning prize after prize for his English prose at Oxford, lived to make a permanent mark on the literary history of Wales.

From Wales also came Herbert Lewis, the Parliamentary Secretary, who when I was a neophyte was already an old parliamentary hand. Lewis was one of those ardent Welshmen who had followed Lloyd George into national politics, and was like him possessed by a passionate love of his native land. There was, however, no element of bitterness or hostility in Lewis's Welsh nationalism. Whereas Edwards seemed to embody the immemorial melancholy of an aggrieved people and never forgot the bitterness of the religious warfare of his youth, Lewis, if he had ever harboured such animosities, had long since outlived them. Though he had gained a good deal of parliamentary adroitness from his experience of the tough contests of the last decade, and was skilled in handling a Bill in committee, he was a sweet and gentle spirit, of whose rare power of eloquence I had no suspicion until I heard him address a meeting of his compatriots at Aberystwyth in their native tongue. Then, indeed, he was transfigured. I had not before conceived it possible that, in a case where an orator has an equally perfect command of the tongues a change in the medium of expression would be capable of effecting so great an alteration in the weight and effectiveness of his speech.

Lewis was a helpful colleague and became a great friend. With him I made an educational tour of Wales, which lives in my memory as a happy experience. We viewed the noble new academic buildings at Bangor and Cardiff, and the great national library at Aberystwyth, with which Lewis was specially connected, and delivered a succession of educational speeches to enthusiastic audiences. In a land so foreign to me it was a good introduction to be accompanied by this lovable, popular Welshman, whose name was so widely known among his compatriots. The Welsh were exuberant in their enthusiasm for education. It was a pleasure to address them. Fairness, however, compels me to observe that at that time the educational standards reached in the state-aided schools of England were higher than those which prevailed in the principality. The last years of Lewis's life revealed depths of heroism and saintliness which only the most intimate friends of his active life could have suspected. He fell down a cliff and fractured his spine. Death seemed inevitable, but Lewis lived on for years, hopelessly crippled, confined to his bed and almost immovable, yet serene, methodical, cheerful, resigned to the inevitable end, his active spirit eagerly employed with old and new books, and his interest in the course of politics as fresh as in the days when he was my first lieutenant at the Board of Education.

My first year of office was almost entirely devoted to the work of my department. Cabinet government was in abeyance, though from time to time ministers would be summoned to the Cabinet room to discuss with the Prime Minister business with respect to which it was thought that their advice would be useful or that a wide measure of assent might be secured for far-reaching legislative proposals. It was therefore possible for me to concentrate upon the tasks of my office to an extent which after the resumption of normal cabinet government in 1918 was wholly out of the question. This was well, for there was much educational work to be done and little time in which to do it. The war was my opportunity. I was sensible from the first that while the war lasted reforms could be obtained and advances could be made which would be impossible to realize in the critical atmosphere of peace. I resolved to move forward at a hand gallop and along the whole front. If I did not strike my blow now, the opportunity might be lost never to return. So very early in 1917 I submitted a memorandum to the Cabinet detailing the deficiencies in our public system of education and the appropriate remedies. My memorandum was short, dry, succinct, a catalogue of points. There were no flowers of speech. I knew that I had to deal with very busy men and that I should be lucky if I could obtain half an hour of Cabinet time. As a matter of fact my Education Report Cabinet was over in less than half an hour. My programme was accepted in principle. The Treasury objections were overruled. When I returned to my office, having carried my proposal for financing public elementary education by a system of percentage grants in aid of approved local expenditure, the best part of the battle was already won.

Finance, indeed, was at the heart of the problem. The cause which had been arresting educational progress in the country was lack of financial support. The engine was reasonably well built, but there was a lack of petrol. Too great a proportion of the burden was borne by the rates, too small a proportion by the taxes. There had been underspending in education, and the time had come when the country should know this. Only a financial revolution, such as the introduction of percentage grants, would enable the teachers to be adequately paid, and a suitable recruitment to the schools to be secured. The plan was that three-fifths of the salary expenditure of the teachers should be found by the Board of Education. The change worked its expected magic. Under its operation the average wage of the teacher in an elementary school was doubled, and, since opportunity was taken later on in the year to introduce and carry a Teachers' Superannuation Bill, which trebled the teachers' pension benefits, the calling was put upon an altogether higher material basis. Hereafter the teacher in the state-aided schools might consider himself to be a member of one of the liberal professions. He was relieved of grinding poverty, of the prospect of a sad and anxious old age. He had just that little margin which makes all the difference between a draggled careworn existence and modest comfort, a margin for books, for travel, for dress, for a healthy human life. The young should not be entrusted to the care of sad, melancholy, careworn teachers. The classroom should be a cheerful place. The state which values harmony should begin by making its teachers happy.

My maiden speech in the House of Commons was on the Education Estimates for 1917, and since its main purpose was to unfold this new scheme of educational finance, it was far longer than any maiden speech should be, indeed I was on my feet for two hours and twelve minutes, an unwarrantable infliction on the members who out of courtesy and interest flocked to hear me. I was extremely thankful to be through with it. The House was indulgent. Everyone was so anxious to hear something which was not concerned with the war, but with the social reconstruction of the country, that my long speech was pardoned. I sat down amid general applause. Later on in the evening Bonar Law sent for me to his room behind the Speaker's chair and observed that I had not used notes. I told him I had learned the speech by heart. He observed that his practice also had been to commit his speeches to memory, but that after he became Leader of the House the strain was too great and that he found it necessary to trust to the inspiration of the moment. Nevertheless his memory remained extraordinary. His last budget speech of two hours was delivered with only one row of figures before him.

Before the House rose for the summer recess I obtained a second reading for an Education Bill abolishing half-time, curtailing the industrial labour of school children, introducing compulsory part-time continuation schools and generally enlarging the powers of the local authorities to promote every type of education from the nursery school upwards. The Bill also combined a number of administrative provisions, extending the powers of the Board over education, in ways which I still think would have been helpful, but which were resented by those who were concerned with local administration. The measure, however, was introduced rather as a *ballon d'essai*, or expedient for testing public opinion, than with the idea of placing it on the Statute Book as it stood. The summer recess was devoted to a campaign for explaining its provisions and listening to objections. I addressed a great meeting in the Free Trade Hall at Manchester, when I met also various branches of the cotton trade, and then tackled the stout opposition to the abolition of half-time which emanated from Bradford. Everywhere the halls were packed and the audiences enthusiastic. One of my most surprising occasions was a meeting of dockers, got together at a moment's notice by E. Bevin on a Sunday morning in the theatre at Bristol. I have never encountered such enthusiasm. They did what I have never seen before or since, rose to their feet two or three times in the course of my speech, waved their handkerchiefs, and cheered themselves hoarse. The prospect of wider opportunities which the new plan for education might open to the disinherited filled them with enthusiasm. Alas! for these good folk. They expected from an Education Bill what no bill on education or on anything else can give, a new Heaven and a new Earth.

One result of this campaign in the country was to make it evident that my bill, as originally drafted, was too drastic for local taste. It is always dangerous to interfere with vested interests. The power which it was proposed to take to group local authorities in larger units or associations was apprehended as a menace to established authority and salaried posts. Every languid and indifferent borough council scented danger in the air, and feared that it might be improved out of existence in the name of efficiency. Protests poured in from different quarters. The Bill, we were given to understand, was good enough, if the administrative provisions could be amended.

I bowed to the storm. The measure was carefully stripped of every feature which might make it obnoxious to the public bodies who would be required to work it in the event of its becoming law. Immense pains were also taken to ascertain the views of employers of labour as to the practicability of part-time education for adolescents. Hundreds of employers were interviewed and their opinions, which were carefully recorded, would fill a substantial volume. Sir George (afterwards Lord) Riddell, who was Chairman of the Newspaper Association, promised me his valuable support in my endeavour to curtail the industrial labour of school-going children on schooldays. Mrs. Humphry Ward, the most persuasive of advocates, was knocking at an open door when she secured a clause in the Bill for her crippled children. Eventually, and as a result of the labours which had been proceeding at the Board for several years, the measure was ready for presentation to Parliament, and in the summer of 1918, after eleven days in Committee, and a desperate struggle against the clock, went up to the Lords, where Lord Lytton, in a series of flawless speeches, carried it safely through the remaining stages of its journey.

To steer a Bill through Committee on the floor of the House is an art in itself, and to my thinking an enjoyable art. The Minister has every advantage. If he knows his Bill and has duly profited by the expert skill of the Civil Service, he should be more than equal to any opposition which he is likely to encounter. He must, however, be conciliatory and prepared for some concessions. I was for instance compelled, in order to overcome the resistance of the Lancashire members to compulsory part-time continuation schools, to introduce an amendment postponing for seven years the application of the scheme to young people between sixteen and eighteen, a concession seemingly great but in reality of little practical importance, since several years would be needed before an adequate supply of efficient teachers would be forthcoming, yet without which the Bill would not have passed. My aptitude for Committee work did not, however, escape criticism. On my second evening, as I was taking a moment's rest upon the Terrace, John Burns offered me some fatherly counsel. 'Young man,' he said, 'I have been watching you in Committee. You don't know how to get a Bill through. You try to make your speeches interesting. Send them to sleep, Mr. Fisher, send them to sleep.' John Burns was right. George Cave, a consummate artist in that branch of the parliamentary craft, was not only persuasive but continuously and pleasantly soporific. I tried to follow his example, for I had greatly admired his work on the Representation of the People Bill, but, as Burns's observations showed, without a full measure of success.

The Education Act of 1918, supplemented by the Teachers' Superannuation Act which was passed in the autumn of the same year, as nearly as possible exhausted the power of Parliament to promote the public system of education. Nor, save that the period of compulsory full-time education has, on paper at least, been extended from fourteen years without power of exemption to fifteen with power of exemption, has any legislative change been thought necessary since. It is not, therefore, surprising that a few years later Lord Haldane should have declined to accept the Education Office which was offered him by Ramsay Macdonald on the formation of the Labour Government. The work had been done. Developments far in excess of the country's immediate readiness to operate them had been made possible under the framework provided by a Liberal

Minister. The Act of 1918, embodied in the consolidating Statutes of 1921, is still in substance our British educational code.

In fighting my Bill through the House of Commons I had hoped to receive effective support from the Labour Benches, for education was a prominent plank in the Labour platform. In that hope I was disappointed. My personal appeals to Labour Benches were unanswered. Though far-reaching and ambitious resolutions were passed at Labour Conferences, many I imagine at the instigation of my friend R. H. Tawney, there was no great show of precipitancy in the House of Common in supporting a measure for the extension of education. Lord Henry Cavendish Bentinck, a Tory idealist of rare purity and elevation of character, was a more valuable ally on the floor of the House. Whether out of modesty or indifference the voice of Labour (the N.U.T. representative excepted) was seldom heard.

The idealist advisers of the Labour party on educational questions were, I suspect, in advance not only of the older Trades Union politicians, but also of average working-class opinion and desires. Hard-bitten old half-timers like Philip Snowden and J. R. Clynes cherished, I believe, a secret liking for the system under which they had been schooled for success. What had been good enough for them, what had so easily fashioned those qualities of fortitude and independence which had brought them to the forefront of the political battle could not be without value. They did not indeed oppose the abolition of half-time but they were not enthusiastic devotees of the change. It was part of their old Lancashire world and they, being good conservatives, were a little sorry to see it go.

I doubt also whether the suspicion of all forms of vocational training which was then so prevalent among the official exponents of the Labour philosophy really represented the sentiments of the average British parent. The professional view was that any form of vocational teaching was sadly likely to be a base device for swelling the employers' profits, more particularly if it were given in 'Works' schools, and that continuation schools were heartily to be supported only if they gave a good general education in the humanities. As an excellent working-class mother of a family in Sheffield said to me: 'I do not want my daughter to be taught cooking and practical things like that. Her whole life will be made up of practical duties. I want her to learn something entirely different and far away from the humdrum tasks of a working-class wife and mother.' There is, of course, much to be said for this philosophy of adolescent education, and it found its place in the Education Act, but I always suspected that working-class parents would really have preferred a more definite bias to bread-and-butter studies, and that in this respect the educational attitude of the Labour party did not represent the real sentiments of the working-class home.

A great step forward had been taken in 1902 when the secondary schools had been made eligible for state aid, and the Board was rightly proud of the progress which had been realized in this branch of public education since that date. But here, again, the expenditure had been on too parsimonious a scale. I made it my duty to secure some half a million of new money for these schools, to improve the salaries of the teachers and to provide them with pensions, and also to strengthen the highway between the secondary school and the universities by special grants for advanced courses for the older boys and girls, and by the establishment of a system of state scholarships which might enable the alumni of the new schools to enjoy the benefits of university life.

At that time the public schools were educating thirty thousand boys. The kind of figure which I had in mind for the secondary-school population (boys and girls) of Great Britain was six hundred thousand. That was a distant goal. A long step towards it has, however, been taken. Already our figures approach the half-million limit.

Another change of a practical kind was of advantage alike to scholars and teachers. There were at that time no less than fifty-five examinations giving access to as many occupations, for any one of which the staff of a secondary school might be called upon to prepare a candidate. Negotiations vigorously and effectively undertaken cleared away this jungle. A single general examination, known as the school certificate examination, was accepted by the occupations concerned as a substitute for the special examinations which they had previously conducted. The many defects which have since been discovered in this established incubus on the young must not blind us to the evils and inconvenience which it was the means of removing.

Up till the later part of the nineteenth century a university career had always been regarded as something of a rich man's luxury. Oxford and Cambridge, exercising by their superb college endowments and great traditions a dominating supremacy, were until the abolition of religious tests in 1871 regarded as nurseries of the national church, and training-grounds for the landowning gentry. At these famous seminaries the landlord, the legislator, the lawyer, and the clergyman received an education in classics and mathematics, law and theology. Though a few poor men were attracted by scholarships the university made no general appeal to the country. The business men in the northern industrial towns seldom thought of Oxford and Cambridge for their sons. Still more rarely did the idea of the university penetrate into the home of the tradesman and the farmer. Whereas the ambitious Scottish peasant had for centuries dreamed of college for his clever boy, such a prospect was far too remote and unfamiliar to enter into the homes of our English villages. Secluded by their high fence of Anglican worship, Oxford and Cambridge kept democracy proudly at bay. Despite the increase in population, the number of students in these two universities did not in 1850 exceed three thousand. The abolition of religious tests at the universities of Oxford and Cambridge in 1871, and the foundation of universities and university colleges in our great industrial centres altered all this. The social texture of the university clientele became more diversified, the university idea more widely diffused, the relevance of the higher learning to the practical needs of modern life more fully understood. Yet I believe that, when the history of our English education comes to be written, no single step will be found to have contributed more effectively to the spread of the university idea through England than the decision of the Government in 1918 to allot eight millions to enable ex-Service men to enjoy the privileges of university education. Twenty-seven thousand students went to the universities with the aid of these state grants. As I examined every dossier I am in a position to affirm that this large body of students was drawn almost exclusively from families to whom the notion of a university career for one of their numbers would have seemed up to that time foreign, if not fantastic.

Though university education in England had been singularly retarded, it enjoyed one advantage denied to most foundations for the higher learning in other countries. No university in England, and this observation applies to Scotland also, had been founded by the State. Our ancient and modern universities were all the outcome of private enterprise. They were self-governing independent republics, free to direct their own studies and to enforce their own discipline. Oxford and Cambridge, until 1917, lived on their private endowments.

The newer universities were from the point of view of finance not equally fortunate. Though private bene-factions had played in every case a part in their founda-tion they could not afford altogether to dispense with assistance from public funds. They received help from the rates and taxes. The leading men of the city and the county were called in to share in the government of the civic university, and though the essentials of academic liberty were preserved the city fathers would occasionally take leave to comment on the proceedings of a body which they helped to form.

The boon of academic freedom was fully understood and widely valued. Even universities which accepted grants from the State would have sacrificed their parlia-mentary moneys without demur rather than submit to dictation from the government. Experience, however, showed that such dictation was never attempted. Yet, despite the encouragement to be derived from the fact, there were many, including the Vice-Chancellor of Oxford University at that time, who were vehemently opposed in the name of academic liberty to the accep-tance of parliamentary money by the two national universities. I became, however, convinced early in 1917 that Oxford and Cambridge could not continue to dis-charge their functions or to cope with the developing requirements of applied science without help from the State. Their needs were crying. Without immediate finan-cial aid it would have been impossible for them to carry on their current scientific work. Austen Chamberlain was fortunately Chancellor of the Exchequer. He was himself an alumnus of Cambridge and the son of the founder of Birmingham University. Few words were necessary to convince such a man of the needs of the two universities. After twenty minutes I left the Treasury Chambers with an assurance of a certain grant of £30,000 a year for each university pending the report of the Royal Commission, which we agreed between us must necessarily be set up.

Such an inquiry, indeed, was long overdue. The Report of the Commission would be a landmark in the educational history of the country. When I was fortunate enough to persuade Lord Oxford to accept the chairmanship I felt assured that its findings, whatever they might be, would be regarded as authoritative and would receive a full measure of parliamentary support.

The administration of the government grants to the universities and university colleges was entrusted, not to the Board of Education, whose jurisdiction did not extend over Scotland, but to a University Grants Committee composed of eminent academic people nominated in the first instance by the President of the Board of Education, but technically acting under the Treasury. The fear that government finance might involve government dictation has thereby been exorcised. The University Grants Committee has not indeed been without influence on academic policy. Having a synoptic view of all the universities and university colleges in Britain, it is in a position to make useful suggestions for the avoidance of overlapping and unnecessary duplication of effort and to communicate to one university experience gained from another. But the authority of the Committee has been by way of indirect influence only, and absolutely devoid of political bias. The successive Chairmen, Sir William McCormick, Sir Walter Riddell, Sir Walter Moberly, have all been men of high academic standing and wide experience of university problems.

The Hallamshire division of Sheffield, being that division in the city in which the university was situated, was willing in the exceptional circumstances of the War to be represented by a Liberal on condition that the seat should be regarded as being again at the disposal of the Tory party at the next election. Nothing short of a world cataclysm could have broken the Tory tradition of that stronghold of true blue opinions. Yet the War changed everything. The support of the Sheffield Tories, led by my friends George Franklin and J. A. Hobson, the one the Pro-Chancellor and the other the Treasurer of the University, was given generously to me and without reserve. I was returned without a contest, my predecessor in the seat, the highly respected Stuart-Wortley, having been promoted to the Upper House, and for two years I represented a constituency which I was not expected either to canvass or to address, from which I received not a single letter, to which I contributed not a single subscription, and which betrayed no scintilla of animosity as to my views. What an ideal constituency, the reader will exclaim! But there is more yet to be said.

My predecessor told me that in the thirty-six years during which he had held the Hallamshire seat he had never once been approached by an armament firm in this great city of armaments to procure for it favours at Whitehall or Westminster.

My next constituency, the combined English universities, was almost as indulgent. Judging by a mercifully slender volume of correspondence my constituents were mainly interested in the humane killer. Larger questions were seldom touched on. And since the member for this new academic constituency was not expected to canvass for support or to address meetings, he was happily free to devote his undivided energies to the work of the Cabinet and of Parliament.

This work was in my case no longer almost wholly confined to education. With the signing of the Armistice the Cabinet resumed its regular sittings and imposed its crushing and multifarious burden on all its members. Henceforward the calls of my department occupied only a small fraction of my time. The chairmanship (in succession to Sir George Cave) of the Home Affairs Committee of the Cabinet, the League of Nations with its annual assembly at Geneva and occasional council meetings in London and Paris, the chairmanship of yet another Committee to settle the pay of the army, navy, and air force, and occasional spells of the India Office during the absence and illness of my friend Edwin Montagu, kept my hands very full. On two occasions I was approached with a view to the Irish Secretaryship.

The prospect did not attract me and I had no difficulty in declining a post which I could not adequately have filled.

For the India Office, on the other hand, I should have felt myself not wholly unprepared, and had the Prime Minister persisted in his original intention of inviting me to exchange education for India in 1918, I should have gladly accepted his offer. A rumour, however, got abroad that I was destined for a new office, and a petition from a Teachers' Conference, protesting against my removal from the Board of Education, made an impression on the Prime Minister. An eleventh-hour change was made in the submission to the King. Edwin Montagu went to the India Office and I remained at the Board of Education. Montagu had a touch of genius. As an Under-Secretary of State for India he had made for himself a substantial reputation not only in the House of Commons but in India. His warm sympathy with Indian aspirations, his oriental insight into the Indian mind, his gift of burning eloquence, enlisted the grateful enthusiasm of the Indian people, and his tour through the country before the War of 1914–18 was a triumphal progress. But though he had his moods of wit and gaiety he was tormented by an unhappy, timid, self-accusing nature. Having owed so much to the friendship and confidence of Asquith he felt uncomfortable at being in the House at all. The faintest breath of criticism caused him exquisite anguish. In a critical debate in the House of Commons on the Amritsar massacre he completely lost his nerve, made a speech entirely different from that which he had carefully prepared, and, overwhelmed by an ugly storm of indignation, suffered a blow in his own esteem and that of many others from which he never quite recovered.

During Montagu's not infrequent illnesses, or during his absence in India where he went to collaborate with the Viceroy on the reform of the constitution, it fell to me to take charge of his office and to handle the Indian question in the House of Commons. The Montagu-Chelmsford Reports established the system of responsible government in India. The Act which embodied them, though now suspended, was a great landmark in history. It was part of my duty to master its provisions and to help Montagu to secure its passage through the House. A few years earlier Parliament would have been staggered by the bare idea of such concessions to the Indian Nationalist movement as were involved in the transference of all the nation-building services to Indian cabinets responsible to Indian electorates. The War, however, had changed everyone's perspective. The loyalty of India in the Empire's hour of peril had evoked a deep spirit of gratitude. Changes which would have seemed too perilous to contemplate a few years back seemed safe now. The Bill, expounded by the Secretary of State in a series of admirable speeches, passed with ease. Though John Morley shrank from the idea of implanting the parliamentary institutions of the West in an oriental country Curzon was well content that the Bill should pass, and the Lords on an Indian question could be relied upon to follow Curzon's lead.

Among the Indian figures who at that time fitfully glittered on the London scene was a young ruling Prince who combined extraordinary graces of mind and person with a secret and deadly disability of character which was ultimately his undoing. Alwar was lissom and beautiful. His English oratory was of the finest texture. Not a word was amiss, not a sentence unconnected. In rhythm and balance as in the musical quality of his voice this graceful youth was one of the outstanding speakers of his age, and his conversation was as finished as his oratory. Unfortunately he delighted in cruelty, and the most intelligent of Indians was also the worst of rulers. When I knew him Alwar was ambitious of playing a great part in the changing fortunes of his country. He would plan little dinner parties for English public men, who might be conceived to influence the course of Indian affairs, and it was diverting to note the elaborate policy with which he manœuvred his approach. When Lloyd George was his guest he was greeted by a faint sound of music, coming as from a great distance from behind gauze curtains which concealed the dining-room, which as it gained in strength was recognized to be Welsh, and was in fact the first item in a carefully chosen pro-gramme of Welsh popular airs. At one time he thought it worth while to ask Montagu to invite H. G. Wells and myself to dinner. On another occasion I was his guest with F. E. Smith. With quiet and intelligent

R

curiosity the jewelled oriental probed the riddles of the new constitution. Not Bryce himself could have been more intelligent. Yet his English guests in India were regaled by the nightly spectacle of a kid being torn to death by a leopard; and his subjects had such ample grounds for grievance that he was in the end removed by the Viceroy from the government of his State. He was an illustration of the degree to which it may be necessary to qualify the famous dictum of Erasmus: *Studia abeunt in mores*. A western education, brilliantly assimilated, had left Alwar at heart one of those unhappy savages whom nature distributes in varying proportions through every race in the world.

Ireland and Other Problems

THE least enviable of all my Cabinet tasks was the part which I was called upon to bear in the endeavour to make a settlement with Ireland. The prospects of peace in that unhappy island, which had seemed so bright at the outbreak of the War, were suddenly clouded over by a series of blunders and misunderstandings. The retention of Carson in Asquith's Cabinet after Redmond had refused to join, the mistrust of the Irish volunteer movement shown by Kitchener, and finally the decision of the Lloyd George Government to extend conscription in principle to Ireland added flame to the revolutionary fires which had burst out two years earlier in the Dublin rebellion and had since been smouldering in the soil. The decision to extend conscription to Ireland was undoubtedly from the Irish point of view a mistake. Everyone on the spot whose judgement counted for anything advised the Government that the measure would cause the maximum of irritation and produce the minimum of effect. Though one of the most junior members of the Cabinet I ventured to support the view of our Irish advisers and to raise my voice against the measure as likely to cause a great deal more trouble than it was worth. There was, however, real pith and substance in the rejoinder that the success of conscription in England would be prejudiced if the Irish were to go free. 'How', it was asked, 'can one call upon an Englishman of forty to serve when an Irishman of twenty is exempt?' Experienced Labour members advised that this was a point very present to the mind of many British working men. The Cabinet then decided to take the risk, 'a battle-field decision', and like most of such decisions a mistake.

That some form of Home Rule should be granted to Catholic and nationalist Ireland was one of the principal planks of the Coalition Government. The Conservatives would not have come into the Coalition without guarantees to Ulster, nor the Liberals without the prospect of establishing an Irish Parliament for the Catholics of the South. As a Liberal known to be favourable to Home Rule I was asked to serve upon the Cabinet Committee to draft the Bill, and at an early stage of the proceedings became convinced that the only chance of a settlement lay in the establishment of a separate parliamentary government in the North. That so small a country as Ireland should be burdened by two Parliaments and two administrations was absurd, but the resolute refusal of the Northerners to come under a Dublin Parliament, or to contemplate an arrangement for contracting in or out, made it necessary. Partition then, however much to be regretted, was at the moment inevitable, but a plan under which each section of Ireland would manage its own affairs was better than one under which the North would be governed from Westminster. The North had its separate interests, sentiments, and aspirations. It stood for the British connexion, for Protestantism, for free trade with the great industrial country across the sea, for temperance legislation. It apprehended that no one of these interests would be secure in a Parliament predominantly ruled from the South. The partition of Ireland was conceived in that spirit of regard to the principle of self-determination which governed the general settlement of Europe after the War.

The type of government to be set up in each part of the island was a matter upon which people felt strongly and strongly differed. While no English political party was prepared to grant the Republic one and indivisible, which Sinn Fein demanded, the trust to be reposed in the Catholic South was variously measured. The rank and file of the Conservative party had always detested the idea of Home Rule, and their feelings had not been mitigated by the widespread sympathy shown by rebel Irishmen to the enemy in the War and by the disorders fomented by the Sinn Fein party at the moment. These die-hards would have liked to resist Home Rule altogether, hoping that the experiment, if tried, would miscarry, and desiring in any case that the self-government granted to the Catholic South should be carefully circumscribed. Balfour, whose thoughts moved on higher and serener levels, thought otherwise. In an essay published in America before the War he had urged that there were only two logical ways of dealing with the Irish question, the way of Union, which he infinitely preferred, and the way of partition and self-determination, only to be resorted to if the Union proved no longer possible. Since the preservation of the Union was unfortunately hopeless, he was prepared to recommend (and here he was supported by Bonar Law) that Catholic and Protestant Ireland should receive exactly what each segment of the island professed to want. Let the six counties be an integral part of Britain, and let the rest of Ireland be cut out of the Empire and set up for itself what government it pleased. This, however, was a proposal very little to the liking of the Prime Minister. Whatever happened Lloyd George was determined that Catholic Ireland should remain within the Empire, and Irish statesmen take their place at the Council table in Downing Street. It was, therefore, on the lines of an Ireland, self-governing but divided, and in any case both as to its Southern and Northern halves retained within the Empire, that it was resolved to travel in search of a solution of the Irish question.

I confess that I was not much enamoured of the Bill which emerged from our deliberations. I took the line that if a Parliament were to be established in Dublin it should be made attractive to patriotic Irishmen by the grant of wide and generous powers, and in particular by a full power to levy customs duties. Far other, however, were the views of the Treasury. While I wanted to do as much as possible, they were anxious to do as little. Their plan for Irish finance might have been well enough had we been merely considering the dissolution of a commercial partnership. As a means of satisfying the aspirations of Catholic Ireland it was utterly unimaginative and insufficient. So strongly did I feel on the subject of the customs that the Prime Minister called for a special meeting of ministers (including Balfour and Bonar Law, and reinforced by James Craig) to convert me. I was left, however, after a long discussion in a minority of one. The Prime Minister, who was secretly convinced that in the end the customs would have to be conceded, was resolved to postpone the great concession and only to part with it for value received.

The Home Rule Act of 1920, however insufficient, was the beginning of new things. There are some facts which, unwelcome though they be, must in the end be recognized, and when the King actually opened the Northern Parliament in Belfast the Southern Irish saw that part at least of the Act was working and that, in any arrangements for the immediate future, the Northern legislature must be taken into account. They were, therefore, inclined to listen to the fine appeal for an Irish peace which the King addressed to members of both races and creeds, and a train of negotiations was set on foot which led to the momentous Treaty of 1921, according to Catholic and Nationalist Ireland a constitutional status analogous to that of Canada, and in all essentials, save that the six Protestant counties were excluded, corresponding to the Irish dream.

I can never forget the harrowing anxieties of the miserable period which preceded the Treaty. The War was bad enough, but the Irish troubles, infinitely less in scale, were far more afflicting to the spirit, and involved the Government which had issued so triumphantly from the fiery ordeal of the great world conflict in humiliations from which it was impossible to escape. Sinn Fein had in fact resolved to snap the bonds with Westminster, and to wrest independence from Britain by force. The Irish Nationalist party had withdrawn from Parliament, a sign that constitutional methods were now regarded as hopeless. A handful of resolute gunmen terrorized the country, shooting down the police, and so effectively dominating the people that murders committed in broad daylight and in crowded streets were perforce left unpunished since no one dared to give evidence against a gunman. By the month of August of 1920 more than eighty members of the Royal Irish Constabulary had been killed. In no case was the murderer brought to justice, yet the assailants were well known and boasted of their patriotic achievements. The whole system of justice was in fact paralysed by this novel method of warfare. The jurors were too much frightened to appear before the judge on Assize. The legal business of the country passed from the established courts to tribunals organized by the Sinn Fein party. A republican government of Catholic Ireland was in fact being set up under the protection of the terrorists. With the prospect of the Royal Irish Constabulary disappearing under its eyes, for constables, despairing of protection, were resigning in increasing numbers, the Government decided to strike back.

If the ordinary courts of the land had been functioning this decision would have been inexcusable. To have a man killed without due process of law is an act of war, not an act of justice. But no government which is worth the name can afford to capitulate to political assassins, or to leave its agents unprotected against assault. The Government was bound to retaliate in the only way open to it, since the courts were closed, the way of force. It was not without cruel misgivings that I gave my assent to the decision which led to the police war. Yet I believe it to have been one of those hateful necessities which in exceptional times must be accepted as the lesser of two grave evils. The expedient of withdrawing the army, which Edward Grey warmly advocated to me in private conversation, would not have met the situation. The Irish troubles raised no military problem. Sinn Fein was not challenging the British Army, for that would have been insanity; it was assailing the police. Only by making this too dangerous a game to be pursued with any chance of success was it possible to maintain the British administration in Ireland, and it was only when they found that their efforts were frustrated by the Black and Tans that a powerful section of the gunmen were ready to treat. When he came to London for the Treaty Michael Collins, the arch-gunman, told the Government that they would not have broken the resistance of the gunmen in any other way. Unfortunately the 'Black and Tans', hastily recruited from old soldiers by the War Office, contained several criminals, who until they were eliminated brought the blackest discredit upon the force.

Before these horrors we happened to be staying with Sir Horace Plunkett at Kiltaragh, the charming house outside Dublin which was soon to be burnt down by the Republicans. The official cause of my visit was educational, but Horace Plunkett's house was an ideal centre for political discussion, for men of all types of opinion gathered under his hospitable roof and torrents of brilliant Irish talk flowed through the house from morn till eve. Among the distinguished Irishmen whom I met on that occasion was Archbishop Bernard, later Provost of Trinity College. Walking with him one afternoon I explained the outline of the Home Rule Bill which the Government had in mind for Ireland, laying stress upon the fact that so far as Catholic and Nationalist Ireland was concerned it was an advance upon any offer hitherto made from Westminster. The Archbishop listened quietly and then answered; 'The Irish', he replied, 'have raised their terms.' I remained incredulous, for it seemed absurd to prefer civil war to a first instalment of self-government which might be further enlarged. 'How much blood?' I pursued. The Archbishop replied deliberately, 'I should say about 500 lives'. On the day on which the Treaty was signed at the Irish Office I inquired how many British lives had been lost in the Irish troubles. The answer came, 506. So at the end of it all, and despite our excruciating agonies, these Irish troubles had cost us fewer losses than were incurred on the quietest day on the Western front.

On the day on which the Treaty was signed I was

introduced at No. 10 Downing Street to Michael Collins,
a burly, handsome young Irishman with a shock of dark
hair, a high complexion, and sparkling brown eyes with
a roguish twinkle in them. He struck me as being an
attractive, high-spirited, capable, violent man, enjoying
a row and brim-full of mischief, but brave and honour-
able, who when once his word was given might be trusted
to keep it. It was plucky of him to sign the Treaty, for
he knew it to be his death warrant, as indeed was proved
in the event. Evans asked him if he would come to the
Palace, whither we had been summoned for a meeting of
the Privy Council. His defiant and resolute 'no' was
a reminder of how little was really changed. Yet in
Collins there was this great quality: he could learn from
experience. 'Where are your thoughts now, Mr. Collins,'
asked the beautiful Lady Lavery, as she drove her
moody Irish guest down Whitehall. 'They are with the
boys of Cork,' he replied; 'I'm wishing they were here
to see this spectacle of might. Then they would know
that they could not beat the British Empire.'

Not least among the difficulties confronting the Irish
negotiators in London was the presence, behind the
scenes in Downing Street, of a brilliant and fanatical
republican who fought to the bitter end for the extreme
Irish demands. Erskine Childers was the son of a British
Cabinet Minister. He was born and bred in England,
had for many years been a clerk in the House of Commons, and had volunteered for military service in first
the South African and then after many years in the

Great War. But despite his numerous friendships and attachments in England he had become, perhaps through the influence of his American wife, who was ambitious of the fame of a liberator, first an advocate of Dominion Status for Ireland and afterwards an out-and-out Irish republican. Working in the ante-room of the Cabinet Childers composed a series of able and uncompromising memoranda framed for the purpose of safeguarding his principles against the infirmity of compromise. When in the end a compromise was struck, Childers, the brains of the irreconcilables, refused to accept it. In the civil war which ensued he paid for his convictions with his life. To many of his English friends the last phase of this extraordinary career has seemed mysterious. Had the strain of aerial warfare, undertaken late in life, ruined his nerves? Was he overshadowed by the violent will of his alien wife? Or did he catch the infection of hatred from his Irish associates? A letter which I received from him during the Irish troubles seemed to betray the disorder of fine intelligence.

To Home Rulers, such as I had been from the first, the Irish Treaty, though in many respects far transcending the limits of what had been offered in earlier days, brought an infinite sense of relief. It involved no sacrifices, it required no courage on the part of the Liberal members of the Coalition to accept the Treaty. It was far otherwise with men like Austen Chamberlain and F. E. Smith, whose active practical life had been largely concerned with the fight for the Union. The courage with which these two Conservative statesmen, having come to the conclusion that concession to the Irish demands was now inevitable and wise, faced the consequences of their altered convictions, is beyond praise. They took a leading part in negotiating the Treaty and resolutely defended their work. There have, indeed, been few finer parliamentary performances than F. E.'s speeches on the Treaty, delivered extempore and without a note in reply to Carson in the hostile atmosphere of the House of Lords. I listened to them from the steps of the throne. Carson was a formidable figure in debate, tall, melancholy, sinister, concentrating always on the strong points of his case, and on these speaking, not indeed with literary grace and finish, but with an intensity of scornful passion and serried logic which dominated his audience, until some strong counter-attack had relieved the pressure of his onslaught. In F. E., however, he found his match. The Lord Chancellor would sit immobile on the woolsack, his face set and sullen as if he were hardly attending to the violent diatribes of his former leader. Then he would rise, and speaking without a moment's hesitation and in flawless resolute English, would proceed to demolish his adversary's case point by point, until at the end not a shred was left of it. It was a duel in which quarter was neither given nor asked.

From the moment the Irish Treaty was signed the Coalition Government was doomed. The Tories would never forgive Lloyd George for having broken the Union. It was in vain that he was still supported by men like

Balfour, Austen Chamberlain, and F. E. Smith, and even by Walter Long. It was of no consequence that the essential harmony of the Cabinet was unimpaired, and that in Austen Chamberlain, the Conservative leader in the Commons, the Prime Minister had a most loyal supporter. On the back benches and in the constituencies a feeling rapidly developed that Lloyd George must go. His services to the country during the War faded into the background of the national memory. It was only remembered to his disadvantage that he had dissolved the Irish Union which had been made by William Pitt, and which the Conservative party, so long as any living politician could remember, had desperately fought to defend. The qualities of the remarkable Welshman who directed British policy for the last two years of the War and the first four critical years of the peace are so widely known and have been the subject of so many appreciations that it would be idle to reproduce here a portrait of Lloyd George. There is, however, one quality, very desirable in a Prime Minister and not always possessed by those who attain to this high office, about which the public knows little or nothing. A Prime Minister must not only have an instinct for the large aspects of national policy, he must not only be an expert parliamentarian, an effective platform speaker, and an astute party manager. It is well too that he should be a good chairman of a Cabinet, resourceful and persuasive in counsel, able to keep his team together, knowing when to ride on the snaffle and when to apply the curb, swift to master business however various and complicated, and swift to form his own conclusions, and having formed them, possessed of the persuasive power or moral authority to impose them upon his colleagues. Now all those qualities Lloyd George possessed in the highest degree. His animated courage, and buoyancy of temper, his gift of witty speech and unconquerable sense of fun, his easy power of confident decision in the most perilous emergencies, injected a spirit of cheerfulness and courage into his colleagues which was of extraordinary value during those anxious years. He mastered all the business, he showed a power of resource in counsel which can rarely have been equalled, and he so handled his distinguished and highly varied team that, when the Government finally broke up in 1922 Balfour observed that he never remembered a Cabinet which had worked together in greater harmony. The Press men were in the habit of saying that the Prime Minister was a dictator. That, however, is far from being the truth. Lloyd George was far too skilled in his management of men to ride roughshod over his colleagues. On more than one important occasion he allowed his Cabinet to adopt a course of which he did not approve. Only at the very end of his long administration, after seventeen years of office, did it seem to some observers in the Cabinet that his grip on affairs was weakening. During the War he was at the summit of his brilliant powers.

One happy and helpful innovation during the War was the institution of a weekly breakfast party at which the Prime Minister would survey the course of the military and naval operations during the past week and invite discussion from his colleagues. The Government was too large, for the Prime Minister wished to meet not only his Cabinet but all the under-secretaries as well, to be accommodated at a single table. The Liberals, therefore, met at the invitation of Freddy Guest at Aldford House, while Lord Derby's house was made available for the Conservatives. Ll. G. was at his best on these occasions. Week after week a brilliant historical panorama was unfolded before us. Nor were the discussions unfruitful. On one occasion Alfred Mond brought to the notice of the company a recent criticism of Helmholtz's theory of light which led the Prime Minister at once to give orders for the alteration of our system of camouflage, and there were other helpful suggestions thrown out round the breakfast table which in time became translated into military action. My own personal endeavour to secure swifter promotion to the higher ranks for the members of the new army was not, however, successful. A visit to H.Q. at Montreuil to advocate this very necessary improvement had no sequel. Though the old professional army had been trained on the experience of the Boer War and was not half a million strong, there were in the last year of the War only four brigadiers and not a single general of a higher rank drawn from the new army. Yet all the talent and power of young England was enrolled in our combatant ranks. That such an anomalous state of things should have been allowed to persist was a confirmation of my brother Charles's epigram written on a postcard from the Ypres salient. 'This is a match between Gentlemen and Players.' It was, as I ascertained in conversation at G.H.Q., a gentleman's scruple which obstructed the flow of promotion from the new army. In order to advance a Colonel to a brigade and a Brigadier to a division it was necessary that vacancies should be created in the higher ranks and that Brigadiers and Divisional Generals, who might not be very bright but who had committed no serious blunders, must be sent home with a sacrifice of salary which the charity of the General Staff was unwilling to contemplate except as a penalty of proved and manifest incompetence. All this was very natural, but it is a bad system which in war-time does not ensure that the best brains find their way to the top.

From time to time a French visitor would drop in to our weekly breakfasts and be placed next to the Prime Minister. As our visitor talked no English and our Prime Minister talked no French, the conversation was carried on through the medium of an interpreter, but so skilfully was this task performed by Professor Mantoux, the eminent historian, who sat behind and between the two great men, directing a stream of gentle murmurings now into this ear and now into that, that the general company was hardly sensible that interpretation was going on all the time. The Prime Minister had strong views about the Englishman who endeavoured to do business in any language other than his own. He held that he was surrendering a natural advantage, if he presumed on his colloquial knowledge of a foreign tongue. He was fond of pointing out that Clemenceau, who had a perfect knowledge of English, affected to be wholly ignorant of the language in public business, whereas Austen Chamberlain, knowing French so well, was tempted by his excellent knowledge to use it in his dealings with French statesmen. There is, I am sure, great force in the contention. However well an Englishman may know French, a Frenchman will probably know it better. Should one, however, entirely confine oneself to one's own language in diplomatic dealings? Surely not. My own practice on doing public business abroad was a compromise; first to establish relations of sympathy and confidence by the use of the foreign language, and then to recur to my own language when it became necessary to state in unmistakable terms what the position of the British Government really was. When I explained to Eyre Crowe of the Foreign Office that I proposed to proceed on these lines at Geneva he was much relieved, saying that there were nine different senses of the adverb *éventuellement*, and fearing that I was one of those Englishmen who knew just enough French to be dangerous.

The Cabinet is a great education. Those who advocate a smaller Cabinet in the name of efficiency overlook the value of a system which enables a number of rising and relatively useful statesmen to enjoy the advantages of

Cabinet training. To listen to Cabinet debates, to watch policy in the making, to be introduced to the vast miscellany of important business which comes before the supreme council of an Empire, and to enjoy the treatment of it by the best political minds in the country is an experience which ripens the judgement as the autumn sun ripens the corn. The more widely these benefits can be shared consistently with the efficient discharge of business the better. My experience is that a Cabinet of some twenty-three members is not too large, for the bulk of the discussion is naturally carried on by the principal ministers sitting round the Prime Minister at the centre of the long table, the juniors seldom intervening unless their special departments are involved. Much, however, must depend on the chairmanship of the Prime Minister. A strong chairman has nothing to fear from a large Cabinet and much to gain, for the growing volume of business necessitates many Cabinet committees, and even in a large Cabinet there is more work than its members are able properly to discharge.

Canada and New England: 1909 and 1924

IN one of my school holidays I enjoyed an experience which in the late seventies was for any schoolboy a memorable event. I met an American. My aunt Julia Stephen told me that I must come with her to make the acquaintance of one of her dearest friends, James Russell Lowell, then American Ambassador to the Court of St. James. A happier introduction to the great American nation could not have been conceived. Lowell was no Adonis. His stature was low, his whiskers were long, but physical drawbacks were at once forgotten in the entrancing charm of his conversation. His gems of speech have long since vanished from my memory. I can only recall a command of spontaneous fun such as I never again saw equalled until I came across G. K. Chesterton.

My second American acquaintance was also a Bostonian. Among my undergraduate contemporaries at New College was a short sturdily built commoner with a shy pale face and retiring manner, a little older than the rest of us, and, since he was already a Harvard graduate of distinction, considerably more mature. E. P. Warren, or Ned Warren as he was called, was the son of a wealthy paper-making family in New England, and himself possessed of a considerable fortune. His learning, especially in the silver Latin authors, was already remarkable, and such as to excite the admiration of Robinson Ellis, the erudite editor of Catullus, and since

Warren was also proficient on the piano and full of ideas on art and literature his company was much relished by the scholarly fraction of the college. Two misfortunes, however, befell this most promising student. The first was that after winning a First Class in Classical Moderations his eyesight gave way, and with this physical breakdown all chance of a First in Greats and a Fellowship vanished. Warren was forced to take a pass degree, and to this great disappointment there was added the frustration of a most cherished design. E. P. had been impressed by the lack of post-graduate work in Oxford, and with characteristic audacity set himself to repair our English deficiencies. His plan was to found in Oxford a graduate college on some such model as that which has since been so brilliantly established at Princeton. He used to talk about this scheme with his friends and infected them with enthusiasm for his idea. His plans were laid. He had set his heart on the acquisition of a site beyond the Cherwell, nearly opposite Magdalen, and there at his own charge was determined, though in his third year as an undergraduate, to build a new palace for research. After consulting Alfred Robinson he settled the price he was prepared to offer and beyond which he did not think it worth going. He was, however, outbidden by a wealthy and powerful foundation, and Magdalen College School now stands upon the site which might have been the Warren Graduate College. This rebuff disgusted my American friend. Warren turned his benevolence to another quarter, settled down in Lewes with a small group of New College friends whom he schooled in classical archaeology, and dedicated the rest of his life to the purchase of gems and statues for the Boston Museum.

The thoroughness and persistence with which E. P. pursued his learned quest were remarkable. His colleagues were subjected to a rigid discipline. They were ordained regular horse exercise, and rigorously sent off to bed at nine o'clock. A major-domo saw to the preparation of delicate meals, suited to scholarly digestions. Liberally financed from Warren's deep pocket the Lewes school of archaeology made notable contributions not only to Boston but also to learning in general. The names of Marshall and Pritchard, two college friends and disciples, became famous among connoisseurs, and there were occasions on which the little New College group outbid the government of the Tsar.

Among the friends whom Ned Warren attracted to Oxford in his undergraduate days was a young philologist of Latvian Jewish origin, who had won the highest honours at Harvard. Bernhard Berenson, when I first knew him in 1888, was a portent of literary and linguistic erudition. He would talk with equal confidence and enthusiasm of Latin manuscripts and of the literature of Arabia and Iceland. Save in one respect there seemed no bounds to his knowledge. At that time he was practically ignorant of art. He had never been to Italy. He had seen few Italian pictures, and it was, I believe, to E. P.'s intelligent munificence that B. B. owed the opportunities of Italian travel which have made him one of the most accomplished art critics of his generation. Only a few years after his Oxford visit he had become an incomparable guide to the Florentine picture galleries, and a master of those refined trains of criticism which Morelli had brought into vogue and by which the long-established repute of many a famous canvas has been disastrously overthrown. His work on Lorenzo Lotto is a masterpiece of detection in art, enough to send tremors of apprehension through the breast of every picture owner in the world.

It was in 1909 that we crossed the Atlantic for the first time, the occasion being furnished by an invitation to deliver the Lowell lectures at Boston. Well furnished with introductions we proceeded by way of Canada, stopping at Quebec and Montreal. At Quebec I had an introduction to the French Minister of Education, a charming Frenchman, but whose name even was unknown to the wealthy Scotch-Canadian banker who entertained us at dinner on that evening. That in a town of some fifty thousand inhabitants (for Quebec has doubled in size since then) a prominent English-speaking banker should not know the name of the French Minister of Education seemed to me at the time almost incredible. But so it was. The English and French then lived entirely apart, sharply divided by race, speech, and religion. Yet no Englishman doubted the loyalty of the French population to the British connexion. Under the British flag the French Canadian was free to govern himself, and to retain all the French and Catholic civilization which he had inherited from the age of Louis XV. That an equal freedom would be granted to him under the Stars and Stripes was not to be apprehended. Though the Canadian ladies dressed after the New York fashions the priests feared the levelling power of the American public school. As for France, the mother country, she had abandoned her kings and her God. The all-powerful Canadian priesthood would have nothing to say to the free-thinking republic. When a priest one day was heard to utter some words of disparagement of Queen Victoria his Bishop removed him from the Dominion to Mexico.

At this time the chief ornament of Canadian society and in the politics of the Dominion was a French Catholic. Sir Wilfrid Laurier, the leader of the Liberal party, would have adorned any European Cabinet. He was tall and handsome, eloquent in two languages, and skilled in every branch of the political art. By comparison with this accomplished French gentleman, whose suppleness and charm of manner might have graced the court of Louis XIV, any English-speaking politician seemed a little provincial.

We were fortunate enough to meet Laurier both at Toronto and at Ottawa. Four recollections remain to me of these brief encounters. I made an address to the Women's Canada Club at Toronto, the burden of which was the larger measure of political freedom enjoyed by the Canadians under a monarchy than by the citizens of the United States under a Republic. I recall a long conversation on the immortality of the soul, conducted on Laurier's side with true French sensibility, as we looked down upon the gleaming waters of the Ottawa under an autumn moon. I recall the pride with which the Liberal enlarged upon the splendid work of the Canadian Mounted Police, how it had established the rule of law from one end of the Dominion to another; how when he was Prime Minister he was determined at all costs to put down lawlessness, and at the beginning of the Klondyke rush had a murderer chased across America and brought back to be executed on the scene of the crime, and I remember also how he spoke of his belief in the gradual softening of the rigid ultramontanism of his French followers. Each of these themes, it might be said, was likely to be agreeable to an English ear. But my conviction is that on all these issues Laurier spoke from the heart. In the largest sense he was a Canadian patriot and one of the founders of the Canadian nation.

That such a nation ever should or could come into existence was an idea abhorrent to Goldwin Smith. This brilliant scholar, once the oracle of Oxford Common Rooms, and immortalized as the Professor in Disraeli's *Lothair*, was now a venerable figure living with his wealthy wife in a suburb of Toronto, an anti-Semite surrounded by Roumanian Jews. He had left England to escape the stifling influence of the English aristocracy, and, after a term of distinguished service to the University of Cornell, had exchanged the lovely scenery of the Finger Lakes for the drab surroundings of a Canadian city. Of Canada, however, he had nothing good to say. 'Politics here', he said to me, 'are nothing but a struggle between two gangs of robbers.' He thought it dangerous and absurd to try to retain Canada within the British Empire. She would be happier and more prosperous as part of the American Republic. What was the use of having a tariff barrier between the two countries? What was the value of keeping alive this backward ultramontane French-Canadian state, which would certainly disappear under the Stars and Stripes, but was only able to survive under a British régime? On these, his familiar themes, the handsome old gentleman discoursed with incisive vigour. Far other were the sentiments held by James Bryce, another famous Oxford lecturer and Liberal, who was then Ambassador at Washington. 'If Canada did not exist it would be to the interest of the United States to invent her!'

Here, then, in the course of a fortnight I found a Frenchman contending that Canada should remain British and an Englishman spurring it on to become American. Both called themselves Liberals, but the Frenchman was in the forefront of Canadian politics while the Englishman for all his gifts and accomplishments had never succeeded in prevailing upon a constituency of his countrymen to return him to Parliament.

The atmosphere of the Canadian Press was at this time thoroughly American. It was in vain that we searched its columns for the latest news of the great controversy which was raging in England over the Lloyd George Budget. Britain clearly was not 'good copy'. The prospects of the impending Yale and Harvard football match constituted the dominant theme of the Canadian journalists.

The two leading Canadian universities are established respectively at Montreal and Toronto. On the strength of two visits I will not attempt to compare them. Each institution has enlisted the service of eminent men who have contributed to the advancement of knowledge, and each has helped in a notable degree to educate the intellectual leaders of the Canadian people. Yet not all Canadians are brought up in a Canadian university. The older American universities stand in the background and tempt many a promising student and teacher. Mackenzie King, the present, and R. B. Bennett, the late, Prime Minister of Canada, were both educated at Harvard. The dividing line, then, between Canada and the United States is neither intellectual nor social. The main distinction obvious to every visitor is that in British territory the criminal law is strictly enforced, whereas in the laxer administration of the Federal republic the gravest crimes go unpunished to the dismay of all good citizens.

Yet despite the national and legitimate influence of the American universities the British tradition in education has some influence in Canada. The Principal of McGill, when I first made its acquaintance in 1909, was

Dr. Peterson, an excellent Latin scholar and a Fellow of Queen's College, Oxford. Dr. Falconer, who presided for so many years and with such success over the University of Toronto, was educated in Scotland. Both men retained in their new Canadian homes a lively sense of the high academic standards which they had known in Britain, and worked hard for their acceptance in Canada. If they did not fully realize their ambitions their failure was due rather to the economic circumstances of the Canadian student, who is forced in most cases to earn a livelihood in the holidays, than to any remission of personal endeavour. McGill and Toronto were full of life and vigour during their respective reigns.

Fifteen years later we revisited Canada. The War had come and gone. The Rhodes Scholarships had had time to exercise an influence, and in Canada as in the eastern universities of America I was sensible of the fact that some of the better features of the British university system, and notably the tutorial system, had begun to make an impression. Our friend and host, Vincent Massey, who had been a Rhodes Scholar at Balliol, showed us with justifiable pride the superb students' palace which he had erected at Hart House. At Hart House there is everything which young men and women can desire: common-rooms, a dining-room, a theatre, a music-room, art-rooms, a library, billiard-rooms, a swimming-bath, and running-track. No British university has provided so generously for the social side of academic life. Yet I gathered that Vincent Massey himself was a little doubtful of the success of co-education, which is a cardinal feature of the Toronto system. Though there is an absence of scandal, there is not that severe thrift of time which the separation of the sexes encourages.

Earl Grey was the most simple, vivacious, and spontaneous of men, and his wife and daughters were equally delightful. But the ceremonial in Government House was carried to a point which I do not remember to have seen equalled even in India, Lady Grey and the ladies making deep curtseys to the Governor-General even when rising from the breakfast table. It is an old and sound British tradition to emphasize by some special outward mark of respect the presence of the King's deputy. The Judges on Assize are received with regal honours and take the precedence of royalty wherever they hold their courts. By a profound and politic fiction criminal cases have been heard ever since the twelfth century *coram rege*, in the presence of the King. The Governors who represent the supreme authority in the Empire are expected to maintain the outward show of monarchy or so much of it as may be tolerated in young and democratic communities. Some pomp and ceremony is, I believe, everywhere welcomed, even in democratic Canada; but were a Governor to be personally unpopular or known to be disloyal to the spirit of the constitution, the ceremonial of Government House would receive its full share of criticism.

Among our fellow guests at Ottawa was Percy Fitzpatrick, the brilliant author of *Jock of the Bushveldt* and a leading figure in the events which brought about the South African War. As we had met Fitzpatrick a year before in Pretoria and as Lord Grey was deeply concerned with South African affairs, being the first Chairman of the Chartered Company of Rhodesia, much of our talk related to South Africa. Could any two civilizations be more different than these which were by a strange coincidence of circumstances gathered together under the British flag on the African and American continents? South Africa, haunted by its colour problem, tortured by drought and cursed by gold, Canada a land of corn, forest, and mountains, watered by majestic rivers and peopled by the two white races whose conflicts have made one of the chief strands of European history. Nothing can surpass the loveliness of the South African landscapes or the beauty of the climate in the High Veldt. A man who has once tasted the joys of the high South African tableland, its quickening air sweetened by aromatic herbs and warmed by the South African generous sun, feels that he is a fool to live anywhere else. Yet who can doubt but that Canadian society for all its intrinsic difficulties is the more wholesomely constituted? Wheat in place of gold, water in place of drought, white men in place of Kaffirs. At the time of our first visit to Ottawa the continued loyalty of South Africa and Canada to the British connexion was still a matter of some uncertainty. The memories of the South African War were recent, and the South African Union, which was only just achieved, might seem to rest on nothing more stable than the unchallenged good faith of two great Boer leaders. Could the British Crown, the sole visible bond of Empire, no matter how shining, appeal to societies so different as Dutch South Africa or French Quebec? Some corpus of common political ideas and beliefs was surely needful if the advantages, incalculable to the British race, of political and religious freedom could be taught. Such a corpus was soon to be provided. My two young New College friends, Lionel Curtis and Philip Kerr, fresh from a remarkable task of good public work in South Africa, were at the moment passing through the Dominion to lay the foundations of the *Round Table*, a periodical which they contrived to make the leading political organ of the British Empire. The subtle bonds of sentiment and enlightened self-interest are now sustained by an imposing mass of political knowledge. As for the regal ceremonial of the Governors it has never been, I suspect, more than a minor factor in our arts of governance. With the republican Boer Lord Selborne's combined knowledge of farming and ability to smoke good strong Dutch tobacco were more important than all the bows and curtseys and laced uniforms which go with vice-regal state.

The motive of our second visit to the United States in 1924 as of our first in 1909, was a course of lectures to be delivered to the Lowell Institute in Boston. That famous New England city, once a Puritan capital, now overwhelmed and administered by Irish

Catholics, was at the time of our first visit popularly
described not as 'a place but as a state of mind'. The
cultivation of Boston was famous. In all the new movements of mind and taste the Bostonians could be trusted
to be in the van. They read the newest books, they
commanded the most recent music, they were hospitable
to the appeal of most religions. In 1910 Arthur Benson
was the reigning favourite with the Bostonian ladies who
sustained the literary tradition of the city. A fine
orchestral society was exclusively devoted to the works
of Ravel. Our dear friend and hostess in Boston was
representative of all that was most distinguished in this
charming society. Mrs. Fiske Warren, gay, lovely,
affectionate, and gifted, had a range of accomplishments
and interests which gave her a position of leadership
among the clever women around her. She had studied
acting in Paris under Coquelin and had worked seriously
at philosophy in Oxford. Like most wealthy Americans
she was widely travelled and at home in many languages.
She could talk of the beauties of Peking and the splendours of Angkhor and was well read in French and
German poetry. A brilliant gift of mimicry helped to
make her the most entertaining of companions. Her
husband Fiske, the brother of Ned the antiquary, was
that not uncommon thing a Boston visionary. He lived
for an idea. His governing deity was the Single Tax, his
paradise the little republic of Andorra where alone that
method of raising public revenue prevailed. This quaint,
utterly unselfish man, an expert, I believe, in the conduct

of business, lived a saintly and dedicated life. The multifarious tastes of his beautiful Gretchen left Fiske entirely cold. Leaving her to lead her own happy life he pursued his lonely pilgrimage, deaf to the economists, and convinced to the end that he had found the clue to the cleansing of public affairs not in his own country only but throughout the world.

On the first morning on my arrival in Boston I walked up to the State House, that admirable specimen of Bullfinch's architectural genius, and finding an old darky at his turn on the steps leading up to the portal asked whether strangers were admitted. 'There are no strangers in this country,' the old fellow replied with a grin. There could be no finer or more fitting motto for the great Republic which, by an act of hospitality un-exampled in human annals, took to its bosom a hundred million Europeans during the nineteenth century. It ill becomes a European to complain of a hospitality which has rid the old world of many anxieties, but the thought-ful American citizen who contemplates the great diver-sity of races and cultures now assembled under the Stars and Stripes is besieged by many doubts and question-ings. 'The centre of immigration twenty years ago', I was told, 'used to be Antwerp. It is now a point south of Budapest.' Hungarians, Greeks, Czechs, Bulgars, and Syrians bring with them new conceptions of life and new problems. The feuds of China and of the Balkans are re-enacted in many an American city, and the crimes of violence which disturb the conscience

– 153 –   x

of the country are attributed not a little to the fierce animal passions which flourish under a Mediterranean sun.

Of all this American underworld, however, we were blissfully unconscious in the sheltered home of our accomplished hostess. Here we saw nothing but New England at its best, cultured, serious, public-spirited. The Irish had not yet taken control and stormed the government of the city by graft. Among the new friends whom I acquired on this occasion was James Ford Rhoades, the historian of the American Civil War. Rhoades was a small schoolboy when the war broke out, and having relatives fighting on both sides came at the age of eight to the remarkable resolution to write an impartial history of the conflict. Once conceived the design was never lost sight of, but since the writing of history needs leisure, and leisure demands money, the future historian set himself to work to procure independence. Entering the steel trade he so prospered that at the age of forty he was able to retire with a handsome fortune, and to take up the cherished prospect of his childhood. The next twenty years were devoted to the *magnum opus*. With the help of a little band of Harvard graduates Rhoades examined every local news-sheet of the period, and produced a book which for the accuracy and range of its information and the fairness of its judgement is not likely to be surpassed. I will not claim for Rhoades that he is a supreme historian. His talent is pedestrian, his book is lacking in imagination and eloquence. But the value to be attached to the just and fair-minded treatment of a passionately controversial episode in national history is very great, and nobody has done more to improve the tone of American historiography than this simple straightforward business man, whose life conforms to Balfour's rule for the perfect creation, 'The dream of youth executed in maturity'. It may be added that Rhoades's History is the first to be written from a close and concise study of the newspaper.

A very different figure was the Prussian historian, Édouard Meyer, who was, like myself, delivering a course of Lowell lectures. Meyer was a great authority on the ancient history of the Near East, and the master not only of all the tongues appropriate to these splendid studies but also of the English language. He was of commanding stature, with a vast capacity for smoke, drink, and food, high animal spirits and a rough loud voice, a great hearty convivial figure. In war it seems to be particularly difficult for professors to keep their balance, and in the Great War Professor Meyer lost his head. But at Boston in 1911 he was full of geniality. We were guests of honour at a little Harvard dinner and called upon for impromptu speeches. The Berlin Professor led off with a long harangue in favour of German *Wissenschaft*. I ventured on the contrary to suggest that the Americans might have erred in following so closely the German model for their universities, and in view of the weakness of their secondary schools might do well to adopt the less specialized schemes of university study which prevailed in the older universities of Britain. Lawrence Lowell, the newly elected President of Harvard, who was present, was in full agreement with this doctrine. Indeed, it has been the distinctive note of his brilliant academic rule that he has converted Harvard into a university of residential colleges and introduced organized academic courses under a tutorial system such as prevails at Oxford and Cambridge, and is there found to do so much for the education of the ordinary man.

November is a perfect month in New England. One still golden day follows another. The skies are blue, the trees are golden, the air is light and nimble, an invitation to perpetual movement. We watched the Yale and Harvard football match in such a blaze of sunshine as in England we may only hope to see in mid-summer. A pious pilgrimage under the guidance of the kindly Mr. Rhoades was made to Concord, where we were of course shown the famous bridge at Lexington where the first shot was fired in the War of Independence, and Emerson's modest little house. I wonder whether Emerson is still read in England. In my boyhood we were all immensely heartened by his enchanting philosophy.

The voice of New England has never again carried so far as when Emerson and Hawthorne, Thoreau, Whitman, and Longfellow were all at work. Other writers there have been of distinguished excellence such as William James the psychologist and his brother Henry the novelist, and more recently George Santayana and Professor Lowes, the gifted interpreter of the genius of

Coleridge. In sheer intellectual ability each one of these writers will probably rank above the authors of the Concord School. But for all that the older men, perhaps because they had a simpler message to deliver, perhaps because the world was emptier of books, and more ready to be surprised, commanded and are likely to retain a wider audience.

Not many years ago Monsieur Herriot, the distinguished French statesman, was a guest in Oxford. I asked him what had struck him most in this his first visit to England. 'Two things,' he replied, 'first your rabbits and second your flowers.' I do not know how well off New England is for rabbits, but the dry stony soil is inimical to flower gardens. Perhaps, too, the impatience of the American people may have something to do with the absence of flower gardens. In any case the lack of flowers is noticeable. We ate our Thanksgiving dinner at the Warren's country place some twenty miles out of Boston. The scenery was like a dainty Japanese landscape, the estate of some four hundred acres full of miniature hills and lakes and miniature trees, all left wild and untended and with not a sign of a garden. Perhaps it is only in long-settled leisured countries that we can reasonably expect such luxuries.

Our intelligent Bostonians were all much interested in English politics. The topic of the hour was the Lloyd George Budget which was universally condemned by our polite and conservative friends as subversion of the pillars of society. Indeed a debate was staged upon the subject in order that my wife might sustain the unpopular cause. I was not privileged to be present on the occasion, but the manner in which she stood up against an army of Harvard Professors (including the illustrious Santa-yana) and showed herself their equal in financial and political knowledge won general admiration. Female suffrage had not yet come in America and the spectacle of a woman capable of conducting a political argument with knowledge and good temper appeared to be something of a novelty.

Index

PRINTED IN
GREAT BRITAIN
AT THE
UNIVERSITY PRESS
OXFORD
BY
JOHN JOHNSON
PRINTER
TO THE
UNIVERSITY